# HANDLE WITH CARE

## *Understanding Children and Teachers*

A Field Guide for Parents and Educators

# HANDLE WITH CARE

## *Understanding Children and Teachers*

### A Field Guide for Parents and Educators

RICHARD BROMFIELD, PH.D.

Teachers College, Columbia University
New York and London

Published by Teachers College Press, 1234 Amsterdam Avenue, New York, NY 10027

*Library of Congress Cataloging-in-Publication Data*

Bromfield, Richard.
   Handle with care : understanding children and teachers : a field guide for parents
   and educators / Richard Bromfield.
      p. cm.
      ISBN 0-8077-3995-2 (cloth : alk. paper) — ISBN 0-8077-3994-4 (pbk. : alk. paper)
      1. Teachers—Psychology.   2. Child psychology.   I. Title.
   LB2840 .B76   2000
   370.15—dc21                                                          00-044334

ISBN 0-8077-3994-4 (paper)
ISBN 0-8077-3995-2 (cloth)

Printed on acid-free paper
Manufactured in the United States of America

07   06   05   04   03   02   01   00       8   7   6   5   4   3   2   1

# CONTENTS

# INTRODUCTION

WHAT AN EXTRAORDINARY ACT OF TRUST—to let go of the little hands we love so dearly, the ones we've nurtured, protected, and educated with all our might, and pass them into the hands of teachers whom we know almost nothing about. Who are these men and women we meet every September? They smile and seem kindly enough. But who are they inside, where it counts? Are they smart enough, patient enough, tough enough, easygoing enough? Will they like our child, take care of her in my absence? And can they teach her?

The teachers feel their own anguish on this first day of school. Who are these children and parents, they wonder as they put the final and inviting touches on their classrooms. Are they ready for school, will they mesh well in the classroom? The new teachers share the parents' worry as to whether they themselves are smart, patient, and just plain good enough to be taking on this job of jobs, all the teachers hoping, too, that the children and their parents come to like them.

While that transfer of hand from parent to teacher can be both comforting and bittersweet in the moment, its power is more symbolic. It stands for the years of education to come, during which, we hope, there will be a strong and effective partnership between home and school, between parent and teacher—an alliance that, more than any corporate or governmental collaboration, holds the key to our children's and our country's future. *Handle with Care* appeals to both teachers and parents in this most-important of joint ventures.

For teachers, I've written this book to share what, as a psychologist who has long studied children, I know about their psyches and hearts, the inner—sometimes hidden—gifts and burdens they bring to school along with their soccer balls and lunch boxes. I share, too, what my working with and consulting to teachers and schools has taught me about teachers' own hearts and minds, their frustrations and triumphs, their brighter moments as well as those more sad and despairing. Trite as it may sound to say aloud, teachers are no less complex, conflicted, and human than the rest of us.

I offer insights to help bolster the two-way bridge that runs between the child's and teacher's worlds, worlds that are all at once as different and same as can be imagined. My book attempts to make safe, intimate, and comforting contact with teachers' innermost demands, tensions, joys, and perhaps hurts, the ultimate context in which their whole beings and ways of teaching reside. The basic truth that most teachers, especially those bothering to read this book, care deeply about their work and students, and if anything, take the child's failure as their own, guides my words. Training teachers to handle students' psychological issues is not the book's goal. Helping teachers to see their students and themselves more clearly in order to teach more effectively and with less stress is.

From a beginning look at what makes something precious to everyone's need to be heard, from the ways that teachers' ears are only human to a teasing out of a classroom's needs, from what makes a teacher to the influence of culture. Language to aggression to sex. From connecting with and confirming children to ignoring and rejecting them. The failure that can lurk in success, and the success that teachers magically, if routinely, nurse out of failure. From student to teacher, teacher to student. From heart to heart, mind to mind. Like toddlers at the shore, we'll pick up every stone of the child and teacher landscape—studying each with care, from the big to little, from the feathery to those that drop on our heads and toes with a thud—all our searching meant to ease, promote, and celebrate the educator's difficult but worthy life's work.

For parents, I've written a book that opens a window into their child's days and experiences at school in ways that most sons and daughters can't themselves put into words. What do they think about in school? What, we'll see together, do they do with not just their happy thoughts, but their less sunshiny ones, the times when they feel useless, clumsy, frightened or inept? From show-and-tell to what they write. From what they need and how they ask for it to what they are asked to give and do and how they cope with that. From their clashing wish to be the teacher's favorite and just one of the class to what school can be and mean for a child of a different color or nationality or language. When a child hates his teacher, or the teacher hates him. Whatever the focus—discipline, hatred, bullying, or being teased—we will explore it in the context of the child and teacher relationship, in all of its subtlety and complexity, richness and variety.

By accompanying their children and their teacher, the parent reader will better understand what their sons and daughters say, think, feel, do, write, and even draw, not only in the classroom, but at home and everywhere in between. They'll come to see more clearly what role they play in preparing their children for school and for helping to support what happens at school. And, just as I hope this book helps teachers to understand parents, I hope equally that parents come to appreciate the demands on teachers and the heroics they perform daily.

For both parents and teachers, I offer a collage of observations, stories, accounts, and reflections—some seen by my own eyes, others told to me, and a few created to make a point. Though I occasionally suggest a strategy, mine is hardly a how-to book. Nor is it a comprehensive text on pedagogy, on teaching, for many fine books already do that well. It is more a patchwork of pieces that intends to stimulate thinking and discussion, and that strives, as a whole cloth, to comfort, inspire, and enlighten. Allowing oneself to not study the book, but to simply travel with it, will, I think, help readers fall into its rhythm and journal*esque* spirit.

"When I discovered that I taught children, not science," a now principal friend told me, "is when I really learned to teach." Likewise and finally, spotlighting all sorts of topics, this book is not as much about the theories of education or psychology as it is about people who just happen to be students and parents and teachers, and more so, about their hearts and minds and the ways they come together in the noble work that educators pursue, often against great odds and much alone, day by day, hour by hour, lesson by lesson, child by child.

## A NOTE TO READERS

I use child, student, and pupil to mean children and adolescents of all ages. If I need to define a child or a group more narrowly, I use other terms, such as kindergartner, toddler, adolescent, or seventh grader. When speaking about children and teachers in general, I go between male and female pronouns to avoid the intolerable monotony of he and she, her and him.

You will soon notice, too, that I've assumed the teacher's voice, writing as if I, too, am a teacher. This, please keep in mind, is neither a deceit nor arrogance. It's to make for a more readable and engaging book.

# ACKNOWLEDGMENTS

I THANK THE FOLLOWING for kindly and skillfully reviewing my manuscript: Mary Mahoney, Lu Gallaudet, and Linda Piecewicz, for catching wayward phrases and discussions that missed the mark; Joan Brégy, for confirming where I'd understood the teacher's perspective and for astutely noting where I hadn't; Janice Desantis, for stressing the authenticity of both teacher and child, whatever the subject or grade level; Gayle Macklem, for sensitizing me to school culture and the realities that teachers cope with; Nancy Nager, for underscoring the developmental complexity of the teaching role; John Raible, for his short but powerful lesson on multiculturalism; Kathy Rubin, for showing me where more was needed or, at least, where it might be wanted; Cheryl Sweeney, for opening my eyes wider to the joy and discovery that sustain the experienced teacher; and Ellen Winner, for spotlighting my need to make clear where I and this book came from, and for whom I wrote it.

I also wish to thank Beth Kephart, who generously lent her literary vision and interest in education to my project, helping me to see my narrative as a whole. Beth offered me the challenge and encouragement to plainly say what I could say and to recognize my inevitable limitations. Much gratitude also goes to Lois Lowry, whose own books have informed my understanding of what goes on inside children, and for alerting me that the book's premise—that psychologically understanding their students and themselves can make for more effective and satisfied teachers—is not without its controversy. To Brian Ellerbeck, my editor, much appreciation for believing in a different kind of book, and for skillfully and patiently guiding me and my manuscript along the complex road of publishing.

And finally, the biggest thank you is to my wife, Debbie, the real teacher of our family. Watching her go from undergraduate education major to graduate student and beyond, from student teacher to seasoned veteran, from teacher of children to teacher of teachers, has given me near first-hand access to the teacher's life. I've learned from her successes and failures and, most of all, from her constant willingness to examine her teaching, and from an openness and humanness that ever touches her students and their parents. I hope she knows that, while she gave me valuable insights into the manuscript itself, the countless discussions, arguments, and thoughts about education that we've shared over the past 20 years are what contributed most to this book.

# HANDLE WITH CARE

## *Understanding Children and Teachers*

### A Field Guide for Parents and Educators

# 1

# PRECIOUS GOODS

DOES ANY ODDER ASSORTMENT of things exist than those brought to a kindergarten show-and-tell? A stuffed donkey missing one ear; a mother and baby penguin, we're told, that looks more like two lumps of clay squashed together. Photographs of family ("that's me"), friends ("that's me"), and things ("that's mine"). French braids, crew cuts, a seagull feather, autumn colored leaves, signs of spring, lost teeth, new teeth, stitches, casts to sign, scratched and bleeding "makito" bites. A coconut from last week's vacation to Florida, an acorn from this morning's playground (also called a coconut by a classmate not to be undone), the other now-found donkey ear, good news ("My nana's coming"), bad news ("Daddy's lost his job"), melting snowballs the size of mothballs, and laments of dried-up turtles and "drownded" goldfish. Stories of recently adopted puppies, drawings to exhibit, balls to throw and catch, high one-legged hops and unrecognizable owl sounds that "Gee, I could do yesterday, really." One-note trumpet renditions of today's hit songs, live grasshoppers, dead beetles, a half-eaten brownie *just for us,* and countless what-am-I-doing-up-here-anyway-thinking boys and girls who, wanting only a piece of the spotlight, stand squirming, with nothing in hand and nothing to say, waiting to be rescued by smiling teachers who gracefully and generously—"My, what a brightly colored dress!"—deliver them safely back to the seated crowd.

And what, in our more fanciful, discouraged, or cynical moments we can only wonder, would eighth graders bring if they had their own show-and-tell? Sealed and unused condoms, stolen cigarette lighters pumped and primed to snort dragon-like flames, pornographic videos of hot babes, emptied bottles of beer, *Playgirl* centerfolds, six-packs of wine coolers for the weekend, used condoms, pills, marijuana pipes, knives, and razor-sharp ninja stars? Sadly, yes, some would bring these things, and worse. But what else might they bring?

A 15-year-old worn and tattered stuffed monkey that still sleeps on the pillow, a beautifully sculpted clay mother-and-baby. Photographs of family ("I can't believe how fat I am"), friends ("God, I'm so ugly"), and things ("I took the picture!"). Pierced ears and noses, new boots made to look old, and their parents' outdated overcoats come back to life. Opened mouths revealing shiny braces, stitches, casts to sign, scratched and bleeding mosquito bites, new muscles and newer curves. Tales of heroism, the next boy's tale of even bigger heroism, hair dyed colors not found in nature, and tears for 12-year-old dogs put to sleep. Bad news ("My grandpa died"), good news ("I'm going steady"), bungled rap chants and moon walks that "Damn, I can do this, really I can." Basketballs to dunk and swish, weights to lift, brightly colored hot candy balls that light a tongue on fire *just for us,* a feeble inch of macramé woven out of a girl's unraveling cuff thread (from a girl determined to show *something*), and still countless teenage boys and girls who, wanting only to be noticed and admired, take the stage, swaggering and sparring, lip-synching and flaunting, until given their teacher's good-natured hook.

Of course, we can't know for sure what junior high students would bring. Unfortunately, or maybe for good and practical reasons, show-and-tell lasts only a few years. But for most children, and the adults they'll grow into, hardly an hour or a minute passes that they don't wish to show and tell. Hardly a minute passes that we all don't want to share something with somebody.

---

There are all sorts of treasures. The buried kind that men, holding maps marked with *X,* have for ages wasted limb and life chasing, or that, fallen to the ocean floor with pirate ships, still bulge with gold coins and shimmering rubies. Picasso's daisies and Beethoven's symphonies are treasures, as are Marilyn's red dress and Elvis's blue suede shoes, especially on the floor of Sotheby's. In the right hands stock portfolios, pork bellies, even junk bonds can be financial treasures. But monetary value doesn't guarantee our heartfelt treasuring.

We treasure gifts of love, the cameo broach that Grammy gave us on our 13th birthday and the pole that dad used as a boy to fish with his father. We don't need greeting card or camera companies to tell us that we treasure memories. Our tearing eyes, the smile that can't be flattened, and a lump in the throat let us know loud and clear that nostalgia, the treasuring of our past, is upon us. Almost any object from yesterday to long ago can seem a treasure, most of all when we unexpectedly bump into it. We treasure these things—the gilded baby shoes, an old newspaper clipping—because they remind us of people, places, and times that we loved and now miss.

We all treasure those that made us, and yet make us, feel good, loved, or otherwise how we want to feel. But tragically, and often to our great pain, many of us treasure people who don't make us feel the way we wish and deserve to, people who may have hurt, neglected, or even abused us. We aren't always happy that we treasure what we do, some of us downright hating that we love what we love.

Some treasures we share freely whereas others we keep secret, softly to ourselves. Such treasures are what fill our diaries. Whether bound in fine Spanish leather or pink-hearts-covered plastic, these diaries serve the same noble purpose as a place where we, their keepers, feel heard and understood, not so alone. Though we try to kid ourselves that our written whispers are for no one else's ears, the diary's flimsy lock reveals our true wish. It is a mere symbol for the specialness of what we live, think, and feel, treasures to be shared only with the privileged few we trust not to hurt us, not to take it away, and not to tell us we hold fool's gold, that what we treasure isn't treasure at all.

---

Don't we feel good, maybe even think we're in love or are soul mates, upon discovering that someone else cherishes the very things we hold dear? And don't spouses worry that their marriage is breaking down when they notice their dreams diverging from the other's? In a perfect world we'd treasure each other's treasure. Showing respect for our neighbors and what they value would be second nature. Yet, for good or bad, our world is not so tidy. Values clash here, there, and everywhere. Such harmonies and friction aren't limited to the conjugal bed. They pervade every crack and crevice of life in the classroom. Some teachers and children just seem to click. Others come together as closely as Pluto to Mars.

Put plain and simple, much of what children treasure violates the codes of the classroom and civility. If they have known a healthy early childhood they may come to school treasuring their bodies and what they can do—jumping, running, whistling. Sitting still at a desk for hours is not what every child treasures or feels good about. And though many children, as babies once able to pee, poop, and eat anywhere, anyhow, any time, have come to treasure their mastery of those same bodies, others have not yet come to terms with the demands of growing up.

Some enter the classroom needing to do everything their less than cooperative way. Treasuring what they see as their personal freedom, they devote their young lives to denying teachers what they ask for, defying teachers' basic treasure—an orderly classroom of responsive students. And school for some children, through the agent of the teacher and her demands, can be an unrelenting assault on their esteem, proving over and over how inadequate they are. When their ideals and those of their bosses, their teachers, butt heads, the resulting psychic and interpersonal battle can wreak the weighty havoc of warring rhinoceri.

And, of course, children are products of homes and parents whose values and treasures may be nothing like those their teacher holds dear or knows are in her pupils' best interest. What a bind these children find themselves in, trying to hold on to their treasures under the watchful, if not critical or punishing, eyes of parents and teachers. At times these boys and girls may be unsure of what it is they treasure, feeling like leaves caught in the going-every-which-way currents that flow between home and school, between their parents and teachers.

The dilemma is no small one for teachers either. They know firsthand the human disappointment of having their treasured wish to be the best teacher they can be stepped on. They know what it's like to be rejected by students, unsupported by administrators, scrutinized by parents, and sabotaged by limited resources as they strive to teach reading, 'riting and 'rithmetic as well as help to raise children with strong character, a perhaps unreasonable but growing role of the teacher. In real life and real classrooms, it can be hard for teachers to nurture and confirm their students when they themselves are being starved and battered.

Coming to know what we treasure is a major task of growing up. Getting to know ourselves helps to set not just our moral compass but all of who we are as persons. Frequently we don't know what we treasure until we lose it, or it's been challenged, criticized, or trampled on. And sadly, there are too many children who, hating themselves, blind to anything good or lovable in themselves, are unable to treasure anything that is them.

Just as the little things that children show and tell begin to tell us about big lives, each of our moment-to-moment inner treasures adds a critical iota of substance to our sense of what we believe and feel, to who we are.

———————

What determines how precious something is? (And I don't mean the "cute as a button" kind of precious.) We usually value what we work at, more so when it's something we want to do or accomplish. Few children experience great joy in cleaning their rooms, even less so when done under their parents' threats. Most take pride when they've set the table at their own doing. But it isn't simply a matter of time and energy. The boy who hastily grabs any old Valentine's card to give his teacher can feel as deeply as the girl who's spent an evening making her own card, her seeming devotion meant more to show off her artistic skills.

We sometimes can judge preciousness by seeing the care that children take with their treasures. The boy who holds batting practice with the 1962 World Champion Yankees–autographed baseball his uncle gave him sees little precious in the ball except its utility for the more treasured opportunity of playing ball right now. When that same child takes a tied and taped swatch of cloth out of a sealed sandwich bag, unfolds it to reveal a dried-up hermit crab, and demands that we wash our hands before touching it, we can be sure we're in the presence of something precious, including a child's larger love of animals and nature.

Precious doesn't have to be saintly, however. A little girl's scheme to get extra cookies for dessert may be precious to her, though she knows it's wrong and will never attempt it. A sixth grader's cheating, misguided and immoral, may be precious to her because she hates studying for herself, or she can't meet her parents' unrealistic standards, or maybe if she does poorly she'll be punished harshly. Wisecracking teenagers often judge their classroom heckling to preciously reflect great wit and social commentary; it also engages the teacher, whose attention they dearly want but are unable to admit is in any way precious to them.

Precious can be what I or you think—*period*. I know one high school student, a boy just learning to take risks with his feelings, whose heartfelt interpretation of a poem was graded as wrong. He read the poem as speaking to loss and regret. His teacher, judging it to be about women's rights, dismissed his view outright. It is not surprising that he gave less of himself and his thoughts to future assignments in that class.

Precious, too, is how we see what we live. Some of our students have grown up in homes where they—under the threat of abandonment, loss of love, or abuse—were forced to not see the hypocrisy, not smell the alcohol, not feel the incest. For these children, even more than the rest, the question *Whose reality is it?* reigns supreme. None of us, not a single one, likes being told that what we think, see, or experience isn't so. If our own perceptions can't be treasured and trusted, what in life can be?

Arguably even more than beauty, treasure is in the eyes of the beholder, eyes that, by the laws of human nature, see differently. But as we will find, this needn't doom us or our classrooms.

---

"If you died, I'd fry you up."

"What?" Gina, the student teacher, asked. She hoped she'd heard wrong. All the classroom eyes turned to the first grader who'd started this startling conversation.

"If you died," Annie said more loudly, "I'd fry you up."

Gina felt her body stiffen and her skin flush with heat. It was the last day of her first student teaching assignment, a year that had gone smoothly and well. Having weathered all the tests and storms the children had sent her way, she'd proved herself to be a steady and caring teacher. She'd even reached Annie, the most troubled child in the class, a girl who, since losing her mother to cancer, hadn't let anyone near.

"Then I could eat your dead body. Yeah," Annie continued with a sadistic cackle and a lick of her lips. "I'd eat fried Gina all up."

"That's enough, Annie," Gina spoke softly, using the gentle but firm stance that for so many months had worked with the girl.

Annie would have none of it. "I'd eat your head and your ears and your eyeballs." She spoke louder. "And your legs and your arms . . . " The children giggled.

While watching her goodbye party fall apart upset Gina, what really hurt was her growing fear that Annie was going crazy and that the year's hard-won progress would be lost.

But Mrs. Thomas, the classroom teacher, knew better. She took Annie by the elbow and guided her toward Gina's side. "And then?" she asked matter-of-factly. "After you eat Gina all up, then what?"

Annie stood quietly, looking at her feet, picking a scab on her arm.

"And then, Annie?" Mrs. Thomas repeated, noticing that Annie had surrendered herself to the student teacher's leg. "What will happen after you eat Gina?" No one laughed.

"She'd be," Annie began to answer, swallowing her words as quickly as she uttered them.

Mrs. Thomas knelt down and took Annie's hand in her own. "Tell us again, Annie. What will happen after you eat Gina all up?"

"She'll be . . . " Annie's eyes welled with tears. "She'll be in my belly."

"*All inside you?*" Mrs. Thomas asked.

Annie didn't reply. Her sobbing face, pushed into Gina's lap, said it all.

"And I'll miss you, Annie," Gina spoke, cradling the heaving shoulders, finally understanding. "I'll miss you, too."

Mrs. Thomas realized that some classroom treasures are not as easy to recognize as the proverbial polished apple. Years of teaching had taught her that some treasures require not sharper but deeper and more patient vision to be seen.

Above all, ownership is what endows the power of treasure, making precious goods precious. While children may enjoy the attention and rewards that sharing themselves with others can bring, they cherish what they say, do, think, and feel in the world and in the classroom mostly because they create it, because *it is theirs*.

# 2

# NEEDFUL THINGS

ANY NATURE LOVER appreciates the clamor of a growing clutch, eight or more chicks all squawking for their mother's attention and the worm she carries. But, as any human mother can attest, human young ones have much more varied and complicated needs. Each day children come to school embodying dozens of needs, primed and ready to surface.

Their teacher shows the children a multiplication problem and what do they need? Several need help understanding it, while others, bored, need the challenge of division. Others needs to master last week's simpler problems and another child, one with fine motor immaturity, grasps the concept but needs help writing the numbers on his paper. One boy, too lost to even ask a question, needs only to be rescued from his growing conviction that he's dumb, while a shy girl needs her teacher to notice the right answer she fears saying aloud. A classmate needs help keeping his hands and feet to himself. Another girl, who is just learning English, gets the math but feels the need to go back to reading, a harder subject for her. Emotional needs—the fallout of divorce, separation anxiety, and the like—distract a few children. And as these bigger needs percolate, so do smaller ones. Runny noses, growling stomachs, and headaches seldom take vacation. Nor does the children's need to worry about practical things, such as who'll pick them up or be home at the end of the school day.

If that isn't enough, even as she contends with the moment's or the hour's needs, their teacher must keep in mind those that are larger and more long-term. As she goes through each day with one eye on the immediate needs of the classroom, she keeps the other eye on the children's academic need to master subject matter, their intellectual need to develop thinking and planning skills, and their social need to learn how to get along and work with others, needs that the students themselves often have little awareness of.

If the awesome and abundant needs of the classroom could find voice all at once, the children's deafening calls would soon drown the racket of the hungriest nest.

———————

Drop us in the Gobi Desert for a week and we'll think only water. Put us on a grapefruit diet and we'll suddenly notice white bread. Give us the flu and sleep becomes all we'll live for. Only when we're well fed and watered, exercised and rested, will we find ourselves looking for people, affection, conversation, fun, books, and the higher necessities of life.

Children are no different. When they're hungry or tired, schoolwork seems overwhelming and is of little interest. Abused children likewise can hardly afford to worry about the perils of a silly mouse when on the lookout for real danger. And when children have a parent who neglects or hates them—sadly, it happens—they can stop caring altogether, disowning any piece of their lives or themselves that depends too much on other people. When children come to school well nourished and cared for, however, from a warm and safe home, from a loving family that sends them off with wishes for a grand day, a homemade we're-thinking-of-you raisin cookie and the certainty that their return home will be celebrated, there's a greater chance that their needs will fit more neatly into the school day. Once there they'll need to play, be with others, accomplish, and learn.

But this satisfying of a child's higher needs can, in turn, create a new dilemma. What happens when a need starts to look more like a want?

"I need help."

Alice's third grade teacher continued helping another child with his math work.

"I said I need help."

"Please wait your turn," Mrs. Marques replied, accustomed to Alice's impatience. "Others are waiting, too," she added as she sat beside Gayle. "You'll be next."

"I neeeeed help. I can't wait."

Alice made noise until it was her turn. But when Mrs. Marques came to her aid, Alice took control, showing off her grasp of the concept and ability to do harder problems.

"You wanted me to see what you could do all by yourself," Mrs. Marques beamed. And so did Alice.

Did Alice need help? By most people's standards, not as much as Ben, who was profoundly learning disabled, nor as much as Carol Lee, for whom English was her new and second language. Alice, in contrast, learned and performed with ease. She was academically at the top of the class. And so we re-ask the question: Did Alice *need* help?

The school principal saw her as an incorrigible attention-seeker who couldn't share the spotlight. Other staff saw her as a selfish little girl who couldn't share anything, whether the teacher's attention, playground jungle gym, or classroom computer. But Mrs. Marques had a deeper view. How awful, she rightly thought, to feel so abandoned every moment of one's life. Though she saw the social greed, she could also see the need behind the want, an insight that fostered her calm, firm, and successful handling of Alice.

The line between what a child needs and wants can blur. Unfortunately, no official border exists. Some children, like the adults they'll become, elevate their slightest wants to grand needs, whereas others dismiss their greatest needs as trivial wants. Learning to tell a child's wants from needs comes with experience. With 20 or more students in their classroom, along with their ever changing needs, teachers face the most formidable of problems, one involving dozens of simultaneous equations and hundreds of unknown variables, far more stringent than the most complex calculus problem.

But the classroom is neither a psychoanalytic couch nor a therapeutic playroom. It's a place where teachers and students come together for the common purpose of learning. In a majority of instances teachers remarkably meet enough of these needs to promote trust and cooperation. Whether trying to manage one child's infuriating and disruptive arguing (*he needs to be heard*), decipher a second's refusal to take help (*she needs to deny her learning problem in order to preserve her self-image*), or break through a third's silence (*she fears what she says will be criticized*), teachers forever process these needs. They ably fill those they can while juggling others that must wait, gently fending off those that are distractions or beyond their powers. Bombarded by these unrelenting needs, all teachers, like all parents, are bound to know moments of frustration when they can't quiet the crying baby, and when they can't figure out why it cries.

---

*Feed us. Admire us. Keep and protect us. Follow us to where we know we must go, while leading us to the worthwhile or necessary places we avoid out of fear, dislike, or ignorance. Caution our recklessness, tame our fury, fire our timid passions, embolden our shaky confidence. Care about what we, our families, our people, and our cultures value. Neither rebuke nor turn us away, but seek to understand our missteps, wrongdoing, eccentricities, and failures, shortcomings that we ourselves don't know the meanings of. Confirm who we are and inspire us to be more, to be everything we can be, even that which our young minds and hearts can't yet imagine. And, most of all, believe in our abilities, our dreams, and our goodness, especially when we cannot.*

Noble imperatives, for sure. This ambitious and admirable list might just as well be carved in Gothic letters on the imposing granite steps that our next generation of teachers climb to their schools of education. But what do these needs mean in plain English, in the everyday language and life of the classroom?

Hold our hands when we're scared. When we've caused trouble, listen to our side of the story before judging us. Recognize the little progress we make even if it's so much less than you want or we can do. Encourage us to face what we must: give that classroom speech, dare to write a story that reveals something of ourselves, poke our heads out of our shells and chance making a friend, allow ourselves to care about or work even if it makes us feel disloyal to our gang. And stop us from mistreating and hurting our classmates before they come to fear and reject us, for our sake as well as theirs.

Forbid the snickers that taunt our mistakes and thicken our skin against the pointed barbs that you can't shield us from. Take our ideas seriously however faulty our logic or shallow our insights. Calm our irritable bodies and accept our nervous needs to fidget. Keep us in harmony, neither overstimulated nor bored. And patiently remind us that *we can* sound out this word this minute, solve that problem this hour, write that book report this month, and grow into adults who succeed and matter tomorrow.

Do all of this and more, so much more, giving us all that we need in every possible and best way, while providing us, too, the most central and important thing you offer us. *Learning.*

---

No teachers can minute-by-minute know all or even most of what their pupils need. And even if they could they'd discover that, much of the time, what the children need is well beyond the realm of the classroom. All and the most that teachers can do is to try their best to see how these needs impact the educating of each child.

# 3

# THE GOOD, THE BAD, AND THE UGLY

RECOGNIZING GOOD BEHAVIOR is easy enough, isn't it? What teachers don't appreciate the boy who laughs at their jokes, hangs on to their words, passes in neat and accurate work, and picks up litter that isn't his own? It's good, we agree, to get As and Bs, try one's best, and write legibly. Should we choose to look to character, we'll be impressed when a child offers half his lunch to another who's forgotten hers or a girl bravely assails her classmates for meanly excluding another child from their recess game of four square. And, being human, we may find ourselves seeing goodness in the child who smiles at us, lends us a hand, and makes clear, in front of the class or on the sly, that he wants to be in our good graces. This latter form of goodness can exert great effect, blinding us to a child's problems or motivating us to advocate for a student who, we know, can do better than anyone else at the school realizes, shepherding him toward new success.

Most of us also feel on sure footing when it comes to bad behavior. Aren't we put off by the child who smirks and ridicules our humor, brazenly talks or sleeps during our lessons, hands in careless slop for work, treats the classroom as his garbage can, and seldom, if ever, does anything we ask? Ds and Fs and chronically not handing in homework, we assume, are bad as are cheating, lying, and blaming others.

But are we as adept at telling good behavior from bad as we think? That a teacher down the hall likes the very student we despise hints at the answer.

"Take it outside right now." Gabe's teacher pointed to the door that led directly to the playground.

"But, I thought—"

"Outside, now. I'm sick and tired of your antics." Gabe set the

frog free and glumly rejoined the class discussion on rivers and wet-
lands.

It isn't hard to understand his teacher's reaction. After all, Gabe was
a hyperactive boy who frequently disrupted the class. But today something else had been going on. Were he with the teacher next door—one
who'd grown up in a house of brothers, had sons of her own, and was
a nature lover herself—she'd have graciously taken the animal as a gift
and a welcome sign of his genuine interest in their unit on nature.

Overtaxed by an unfair number of problem students, one teacher is
happy to nurture and reward a shy girl's deference, whereas her less-
stressed colleague pushes the same girl to assert her strong and capable
opinions without so much fear of others' disapproval. What one teacher
admires as a boy's strong leadership strivings, another sees as bullying
power-hunger that needs taming. It's relative.

That bad behavior often has its good reasons only confounds our
analysis. We may learn that it's Johnny's isolation, not his wish to be a
criminal, that makes him vulnerable to the influence of wild friends. To
ignore that, and openly put down the few people he counts on, will deter
his finding better companions. Perhaps, if we're open to it, we'll discover
that a girl doesn't listen to us because no one listens to her, or a boy
bothers his classmates and us with unwanted, unremitting, and unhelpful
helpfulness because he feels useless.

Bad behaviors, particularly those in the public arena of the classroom, ofttimes ask for something, something the meaning of which may
be worth listening for. While we frequently need to take firm and sudden
action to stop something bad, it almost never does harm to wonder
aloud, or to ourselves, *Where does that bad behavior come from? What
does it seek? What does it distract from? What does it soothe? Is it really as
bad as it looks?* Looking for the goodness in the bad can be the first step
toward reforming and transforming our students.

---

The Life of Riley. The Golden Age of Childhood. A carefree time
of glorious rainbows and winking suns, golden rays falling on pastel flowers, the innocence as pure as the image, the joy as vivid as its technicolor.
A time for good thoughts, a time for happy thoughts. Painted ponies,
honey bears, and sugar plum fairies. That, so some believe, is what preoc-
cupies a child's mind. But the rest of us only wish that could be true. If
only a child's life, for any child, were that sweet and easy.

In truth a child's experience of childhood is more labored and per-
plexing. Though boys and girls try their hardest to wield power—throw-

ing tantrums, digging their heels in, insisting on that blue cereal bowl—there isn't much of importance in their lives that they actually control. They can't dictate the comings and goings of their mothers and fathers, whether they divorce, get married in the first place, or put them up for adoption. They have no say in loved ones' falling ill, moving away, or dying—losses that can slam a person early in life. No ones asks these boys and girls if they wish to be born to affluence or poverty, in the country, city, or suburbs. Nor are they given a vote on the parents they get. What child would choose parents who are undependable, abusive, neglecting, self-centered, or who didn't even want her?

The world as it is today doesn't do much more to promote whatever purity of childhood there is. While the demands of life have remained constant, no one can miss the ways in which our society has changed. Random hatred and recreational violence pervade our streets and schools. Saturating our culture, sex assaults our children on the television, at the movies, through the Internet, in their music and magazines. Many seventh graders know more than their parents; too many high schoolers have done more than their parents; and many younger children, especially those living with older siblings, see and hear far too much.

While informative, the unnatural immediacy and everywhere*ness* of the media and news swamp children and their families with images of human catastrophe and cruelty. Any half-way intelligent child soon learns that nuclear missiles, nuclear spills, terrorist bombings, germ warfare, airplane and car crashes, cancer, AIDS, stabbings, rapes, and stray bullets can get him any minute or, at least, has gotten someone somewhere. Even sadder, many children have firsthand already witnessed or lived horrors of their own.

But even if such pressures and trauma can be avoided, the plain old garden variety of growing up is enough to stress most children. For as it offers with the one hand the rewards of competency, privilege, and independence, it inevitably takes away with the other, demanding that children forsake the things dearest to them: pacifiers, pooping and peeing wherever and whenever, and endless cuddling, affection, and indulgence.

All of this is just the beginning and a piece of the life that children bring along wherever they go, even to their classrooms.

---

There are too many girls and boys who come to school mistreated, whose thoughts and feelings have been corrupted and tainted through no fault of their own. Distracted by their fears and trauma, and guarded lest it happen again, they need their energy to merely keep their heads above water. The cellophane-thin scar atop their psychic wounds barely protects the raw vulnerability. Few places in their lives and their classrooms feel safe. It's easy to understand why such a child has jaded fantasies, why she may see danger everywhere, even where it doesn't exist, even, perhaps, in our own benevolent gestures or those of her classmates.

But it's not only the brutalized or grossly neglected child who knows such terror and nightmares. Every thinking child has thoughts and feelings that are less than warm and fuzzy, feelings that can leave him feeling unimaginably despairing, frightened, and doomed. We know from our own lives that we don't have to be psychotic to feel crazy, orphaned to feel wholly abandoned, abusing to feel abusive, or even abused to feel mistreated.

Like everyone else's, a child's mind has a mind of its own, going there then here, wherever it chooses, weaving in and out, between what's conscious and what's hidden, what's intended and what seems out of his control, and what's fact and fancy.

"Write a poem about this tree," a teacher begins his lesson on forests. But what do those 54 eyes see?

Many see nothing more than a mighty tree. Some wonder if they'll live to be that old. Two boys secretly imagine cutting it down, one enjoying his dream of being a Paul Bunyan, the second wishing he could destroy all of nature. Knowing that trees help make oxygen, a girl with asthma thinks of the rain forest, seeing its and her survival as one and the same. In his mind's eye one fun-loving boy climbs high into the tree as his friends look for him in vain. Another child rubs his wrist, the one he broke falling out of a small apple tree on his aunt's farm. While they think and write, all sorts of thoughts and feelings run through the children, who are too lost in themselves and what their teacher says to notice that the new girl has withdrawn into herself. For reasons she'll never share with them, she can only focus on a black hole in the tree's enormous trunk, a hole in which she's certain a baby squirrel cries for its mother.

And so, as they listen and work, children are enlivened, sometimes bombarded, by what they think and feel, by their reaction to what they hear as well as what they see, feel, and even smell. As they mature they'll learn to distinguish their inner life from that on the outside, and to manage the more agreed upon realities of the classroom and life beyond even as their feelings and fantasies go wild or push them in other directions. This inch-by-inch, step-by-step learning to live more comfortably between the more agreed upon outer world and the powerfully real inner one can't help but pervade the classroom, for it is a lifelong exercise, the quintessence of human existence.

———

There's only one thing worse than feeling hopeless, helpless, and worthless. And that is feeling hopeless, helpless, worthless, *and alone.* The sense that we're all alone with our hurts and our selves can be the most painful experience of life, and sometimes can be much too much to take.

While on the surface our remarking *You feel so stupid* to a child may seem heartless and destructive, it can be the most buoying reply to a child who, unable to grasp a math concept, has confessed his being the stupidest person in the universe. Our simple remark shows that we get it, that we hear what he believes and what tortures him so, and that we can take it, meaning his momentary hatred for himself. Though our telling or showing him how smart he is will soon have its place, right now it risks making us appear shallow and foolish, once again leaving him alone with his self-disparaging sense of failure. Once he feels heard, feeling respected and maybe even loved, he'll be able to hear other truths, such as ways in which he's more capable than he can see as well as ways he detours his own learning.

Children who are sad, angry, or upset for good reason don't need our cheering or distracting them from what they're right to feel. While the classroom equivalents of rodeo clowns are sometimes needed to divert a raging steer or quell a brewing commotion, they seldom have a place in a child's heartfelt reacting. *I'm sure your mother will be fine. I'm sure she won't die* doesn't help a child who worries about her mother's serious illness. She knows the score. False reassurance reassures little, and risks abandoning the child in her time of need, in the time when she needs to hear *You are so afraid, and so worried,* or nothing more than the breathing of teachers who know they can't say anything to make it all better and who understand why she's having trouble doing her seat work that day.

When feeling held and stuck by, it's astonishing all that a child, or any one of us, can manage and overcome. Feeling understood is arguably the most profound feeling a person can know. But, that teachers may grasp a child's plight or hear what he tries to tell them doesn't imply that their job is to be a therapist or that they must devote endless and unavailable time for one-on-one queries into the students' emotional states. That, in fact, would probably do more harm than good, deterring more than promoting functioning in school. It means only that the more teachers can confirm and acknowledge what they inevitably see and hear, neither devaluing nor dismissing it, the more they'll reach each child with what it is they themselves want heard and learned.

---

There is almost nothing to compare with the mix of bad and good, bright and dark, whimsical and profound, fantastic and mundane, that is a healthy child. By striving to understand as best we can, to hear what their acts, words, and bodies are telling us, we guard against our pushing away the child's thoughts and feelings. For when we push away what a child thinks and feels, we push away a child.

# 4

# OUR EARS ARE
# ONLY HUMAN

W E ALL KNOW that our students, like ourselves, want to be heard. Nor is it news that we want to hear them. For even the most motivated teachers, however, delivering the goods is often easier said than done. What gets in our way? What trips up our best efforts to hear what our pupils tell us?

Karen Adams ran her kindergarten class with the efficiency of the Swiss railway. The activities, always well prepared, started and stopped pretty much to the minute. Her young students were the best behaved in the school. They silently marched to the lunch room, the gymnasium, or even back from the free-for-all of recess. And this was no charade. Whatever time or day, parents and colleagues who came to her room unannounced found a classroom that was neat and quiet.

As any parent or teacher can imagine, Ms. Adams's class didn't get to where it was by accident. Only a second-year teacher, she worked hard. She got to school at sunrise to photocopy worksheets and test-drive new projects and she seldom left before late afternoon. Evenings and weekends were devoted to lesson planning and other schoolwork. The children's remarkable orderliness, however, came at a price even higher than her long and dedicated hours.

Her principal, while valuing the young teacher's work ethic and ability to establish structure, received too many calls from parents who complained that their children were unhappy in Ms. Adams' class and were coming home stressed and in tears. As adept as she was at exercising authority, that's how unable she was to deal with the occasional child who didn't fall in line. Parents sensed that their conferences went badly, too, despite her meeting willingly, promptly, and with lots of detailed and well-documented information about their child.

Ms. Adams cared terribly about her pupils. Their problems tormented her and she worked to understand them with the same vigor she brought to her teaching. But ultimately what brought her insight was not more work, but a personal experience: her not being invited to a fellow teacher's wedding. "I can't believe I forgot," the newlywed told her. "Maybe I thought you'd be too busy to come."

The hurt of being left out and forgotten reminded Karen that she'd been too busy for a lot of things, including her students. She couldn't hear what they said—their upsets, their joyous noise, their frustrations— because she'd been too busy following her agenda, taking care of the business she judged came first. Set on her mission of maintaining control, understanding its being a requisite to education, she found that the children's spontaneity and her own came to look more like a threatening enemy and less like gifts to breathe life into the class. Armed with this self-knowledge, realizing that her need for control belied a deep-seated fear of losing it, Ms. Adams eased up just enough on her students and herself. She soon found herself reaching and enjoying the children and her work more than she'd ever dreamed of; and they, her.

---

Mr. Racker and his seventh grade-English class were correcting their vocabulary quizzes when the principal's voice came over the intercom. "I have some tragic news to convey," she began, before reporting that the space shuttle had exploded. Ken broke into laughter. "What's wrong with you!" Mr. Racker bellowed. "I used to think a lot of you, but I guess I'm not a good judge of character." The class watch in stunned silence as their teacher, with uncharacteristic disgust, told Ken to do them all a favor and just get out. Eyes watering, the boy gathered his things and walked out.

Only after cooling down later that day did Mr. Racker learn, from Ken's best friend, the reason for the teenager's confusing response to the news. The boy had expected the bulletin to announce that a favorite elementary school teacher, one he knew was quite ill, had died. He'd felt enormously relieved to hear that the person who died was someone he didn't know. But that pleasure was short-lived, soon bringing guilt, shame, and the nervous giggling.

Flooded by the false belief that he'd been wrong, that his liking and respect for one of his strongest students was errant, Mr. Racker had neglected to ask for, much less hear, what turned out to be Ken's anything but evil thoughts.

*Sometimes, we're so sure we know what our students think and feel, we forget to ask.*

"I can't stand myself, that's why," 13-year-old Marie answered to her teacher's after-class question as to why she'd recently grown sullen, neglected her work, and dropped out of the school newspaper club. "I'm just so plain and ugly."

"But you're adorable," Ms. D'Angelo replied, dumbfounded this attractive and bright child could see herself any other way.

"Why don't you open your eyes and see what I really am?" Marie shot back.

"And you're smart. Your made honor roll last quarter."

"That's not the point." Marie fled the room.

Ms. D'Angelo was right. Marie had no obvious reasons to feel anything but intelligent and attractive. But she had other reasons. Puberty was changing her. Her petite body was growing bloated and clumsy. Social demands and burgeoning sexuality were shaking her self-confidence. Pained to see her star pupil suffer so, Ms. D'Angelo tried to boost the girl's self-confidence by making her see herself more clearly. She failed.

That afternoon, however, walking back to her room, Ms. D'Angelo noticed what appeared to be the old Marie cheerfully walking and talking with the school custodian who mopped the cafeteria floor. Later that day, Ms. D'Angelo went to see the custodian. "What did you say to her?" she asked. The custodian shrugged. "What's there to say? The kid told me how miserable she was and I listened." Seeing Ms. D'Angelo's interest, the custodian went on. "With my first girl, I did all the talking. It's taken me three of them to get it right. Now I'm lucky to get a word in edgewise."

*Sometimes, what we want to believe about our students isn't at all what they believe about themselves.*

"Will our hearts clog up, too, and stop?" one second grader asked on behalf of her classmates. Several of the children felt their chests to make sure their hearts still beat.

"Why don't we finish our discussion tomorrow," Mrs. Clayman wisely said, noting the furrowed brows around the room.

The class discussion had begun innocently enough while the students read a story about a fatherless child. "What happened to him?" one boy asked. To her own and great regret, Mrs. Clayman, thinking about her own father's heart attack and nervous about her own high blood pressure and cholesterol, answered directly. Maybe he had a car accident, or was sick, she supposed aloud. Maybe he had heart disease, she added, proceeding, as the children seemed to request, to explain what that meant in terms of blood vessels, blood lipids, and blood flow. *Thank God I muzzled myself before bringing up cancer,* she thought. Recognizing that her own worry had led the way, seeing that all they wanted was to have their worry about their fathers and themselves heard and allayed, Mrs. Clayman returned to the children.

"You didn't like the father's being gone, did you?" she asked with calm authority. *No, we didn't,* their reactions told her, their faces now relaxing.

*Sometimes, we confuse our own worries with those of our students.*

———————

There's an old joke about a man who holds a delusion that his body is being taken over by ants. "Doc, Doc, you gotta help me," the man cries to his psychiatrist as he desperately brushes the imagined insects off his suit. "Well, don't get them all over me," the psychiatrist rebukes, sending the man on his way. Not that funny. But the joke, unknowingly I'm sure, carries a worthy message. It's the man's fantasies and feelings, not the bugs, that his psychiatrist can't take.

The feelings can be clear and ominous. Imagine sitting with a roomful of children one of whom has just returned to school after his mother's death. The grief and agony of that one child would be enough to overwhelm almost anyone. Many of us would understandably try to avoid the sadness. It would be a courageous teacher, indeed, who could bear the collective anguish of the class, who could cope with the feelings of one motherless child and 22 others scared to death that they, too, could lose a parent. Or the feeling can be more hidden, but no less challenging, as when a male junior high school English teacher, unaware of his colossal fear of homosexuality, discourages a gay and gifted student from pursuing his interest and talents by unconsciously grading him down, overly critiquing his essays, and subtly dissuading his joining the school's writers' club.

As common as it is human, we frequently are most unable to hear feelings that resonate with the dislikes we hold for ourselves, especially dislikes that we've yet to come to terms with. "Get used to it. Life isn't a party," may be true. But our taut remark reveals something of us, too. Why are we so defensive when student after student seems to evaluate us as mean-spirited and too hard? Maybe they touch something we know but can't accept. Haven't our spouses, children, and so many others told us the same thing? Only when we begin to acknowledge what is in us, and what we don't approve of in us, can we make the decision to change—in that case, for example, to become kinder to our students. Even when we are unfair, impatient, unreliable, stubborn, inflexible, too easy, (fill in the blank), we don't like being told so, and we often shoot the messenger, or at the very least we try not to listen to what he says.

Sometimes it's our own needs that obstruct our dealing with the children's. Our need to be admired can lead us to think best of the students who pay us the tribute we crave. Our need to be loved can lead us to give most to the pupils who shower us with their affection and gifts. Our need to be helpful and needed can lead us to work hardest for those who make clearest their need for us, and whose progress most rewards our efforts. Though some children profit from our needy biases, from the lopsided attention we send their way, others lose out.

The ways in which our needs make themselves known in the classroom are limitless. Whatever they are, and whatever forms they take, they are always worth observing and tracking. Though teachers, no less than the children before them, are needful too, that doesn't have to do bad, and more times, does great good. For isn't it also a basic need that moves teachers to teach and do all the helping of children that they do?

---

Let's try a social experiment. Let's take a hundred people to Boston and set them loose. Watch them.

The artists find the museums of art while the scientists seek out the Museum of Science. The shoppers hit the Plaza Mall, the readers browse Cambridge's book shops, and the collectors go antiquing in the South End. The athletes run our marathon and row the Charles while the sports fans rush to Fenway and the Fleet Center. The fashion conscious, music lovers, financiers, and historians go in every direction, seeking what interests them, as do the architects, retired sailors, and marine biologists. The star-gazers take in the Planetarium while the navel-gazers meditate at a Buddhist sanctuary and the horticulturists delight in the Arboretum and Public Gardens.

Free to do what they want, most of the hundred go where no one else goes. But even when two or three elect the same destination, such as the Museum of Art, it's unlikely they will travel together once there. One likes painting, another drawing. Ancient or modern, mommies or

Monet. Visitors to the Science Museum are in no more agreement. Like the waves in the water tank they rush through the museum's tight entrance, spreading out to a fan, running to the lightening rods, baby animals, dinosaurs, and computer laboratory. And even were we to interview those crowded around any particular exhibit, we'd find that what each person sees and learns varies.

But our study is far more complicated. Our tourists differ in other important ways. The fit walk and bike everywhere while others, fearing the rain and the sun, prefer cabs. The more focused and pensive spend the day at one attraction, slowly moving through its halls, watching every presentation, reading every inscription. Those needing more novelty speed-dial the city, completing Fodor's three-day itinerary in less than one. Wanting only to see as much of Boston as they can, some skip meals or grab coffee and granola on the run while some eat their day through a tour of ethnic restaurants. Our tourists approach the day in unique ways that, more than any trolley driver or museum guard, guide how they see, hear, smell, taste, feel, and experience their visit to Boston, and probably the whole of their lives.

When teachers walk into a class of children, they face just as assorted a group. Children who can sit for hours; children who ceaselessly tap their toes, twirl their hair, and tap their pens—that is, when they aren't calling out or falling out of their chairs. Those who learn best by hearing or seeing. Natural-born readers, the dyslexic, and everything in between. The musically, artistically, and athletically, talented or challenged. Writers, talkers, thinkers, watchers, doers. Some who are creative types versus classmates who thrive by doing what they know over and over. Boys contented by sameness and routine; boys, ever prone to boredom, who hunger for novelty. Risk-takers and safety-seekers. The socially eager and the shy. The intellectually confident and the tentative. Leaders and their followers. The emotionally intelligent and the less so. Truth-keepers and crooks. Independent workers and those wanting, if not needing, the help of others. Children who are most comfortable in the abstract, those who like the concrete, and the rare ones who smoothly commute between the two. The organized and the scattered, the thoughtful and the impulsive. Left brain'rs, right.

Astonishingly, teachers teach every one of these children, however dramatically they and their traits may clash with the students and theirs. Whether the child's world view is to see patterns and shapes, think in terms of numbers, hear harmonies, find cause and effect, sense movement, want just the facts ma'am, or work to help everyone get along peacefully, teachers somehow relate to it, and grasp that as the context and cognitive lens through which the child experiences and learns, whatever the subject. Good teachers strive to appreciate the good, bad, ugly, and *the different* of each and every student.

---

There are many reasons why we can't always hear the children's messages and see where they are. As humanly erring teachers we are forever doomed to miss much. But we can ever work at listening and seeing better. Being open to what is in our own hearts and minds, and to what is our own preferred way of learning, may be the surest route to appreciating what is in our students' hearts and minds and to comprehending how they see our classroom, our lessons, and their worlds.

# 5

# TEACHERVISION

ALMOST EVERY ASPECT of our being profoundly colors, if not distorts, what we see and experience. All of us. That our perception of our students, our TeacherVision, is equally imperfect and subjective should hardly surprise us. But it should concern us. For as in any enterprise, the poorer our sight, the more likely we are to trip and fall. Truer than any gospel, how we teach our students has everything to do with how clearly we see them. But we can't change something until we know what it is.

TeacherVision is neither a new educational cable station nor an eye condition caused by peering over half glasses. It's the sum of the ways that teachers look at, feel about, and understand their students, themselves, and their teaching; the whole of their perspective, throughout their career and at any second. The impressive stuff that even 91-pound teachers seem to haul daily—the shoulder bag bursting with tests, composition books, and worksheets; the produce carton stacked sky high with books and assorted jars and cans for a science project—a load heavy enough to break any steelworker's back, is but a feather and a peanut compared to all that teachers bring to their teaching. Consider what they carry to school.

## INFORMATION

A new approach to teaching the concept of negative numbers that intrigued them at last week's conference. The names and capitals of break-off nations they memorized over the weekend to prepare for the upcoming section on world geography. The five children's novels they read to better understand their students' book reports. The number facts, grammar rules, and general wealth of data they've spent a lifetime accumulating, as well as that which they must learn and re-learn in order to master and teach their subjects competently. But knowing about cloud types and the past perfect tense is not the only information they possess.

How and why some children learn best by seeing, others by listening, and those with short attention spans by having more structure. How working only for candy and stars can imperil children's learning to work for their own sake and satisfaction. What distinguishes a non-verbal learning problem from other sorts. Ways to teach reading to precocious readers, ways to teach reading to the struggling, and ways to tell which is needed. When teachers enter the classroom they come with the understanding and wisdom they have about children and learning. Though they get what they know from courses and books in education, from what they read, and from their fellow teachers, other professionals and parents, they learn most from the students, who relentlessly teach them who they are, what they need, and how best to give it.

## EXPERIENCE

Perhaps too obvious to mention, teachers also bring all that they've lived through, from their first wail to the moment that just rushed by reading this sentence. Their own good, bad, and ugly; the joyous and traumatic, the expected and sudden, the pedestrian and exalted. Though they may vividly recall the big days—the birthdays, the first kisses, the graduations—it's probably the years of days in between that have affected them more and shaped who they are.

What has life been for them? Were they loved, hated, or neither, living in a home where their parents, busy with their own lives or unable to care more, seemed indifferent to them? Were they encouraged and celebrated, or were they put down and told, maybe convinced, that they'd never amount to anything? Was their curiosity nurtured and relished, their childhood enriched and stimulated? Or were they liked best when they made no noise, when they sat quietly in their rooms, asking for little but to watch television for hours? Were they raised to trust the world, and their own teachers, or to suspect them of trying to hurt or con them?

And what was their school life like? Were they good students or bad? Well behaved or misfits? Where did they spend most of their 12 years: in the teacher's approving glance, in her doghouse, in the principal's office? Did learning come easy or hard, early or late? Did they sail into teaching on a sea of accomplishments or only after overcoming personal defeats and finding their calling later in life?

Of course, one experience seldom makes a person. And the effects of experience are neither singular nor one way. One woman copes with her deprived childhood by bitterly never giving to others, resenting anything anyone gets—especially her kindergartners, whom she sees as overly coddled by their parents. Another woman, coming out of a similar home, finds her happiness in giving others the love and caring she never knew, taking her greatest joy in seeing her young pupils parented well. For many teachers it is the misery they once knew in school or learning that propels their devotion to their students today. The caretaking we got from parents, teachers, and others can become the teaching ideals to which we aspire or the horror of horrors that we desperately work to be nothing like. No less than parents, we can see and use our students to repair, reenact, recreate and undo our own childhoods in good and bad ways.

### BELIEFS

Teachers' personal philosophies inform their vision. Some see the world and people by way of their religious convictions, their teaching their way to serve God, humbly helping to enable their and His children to be His good servants. Others, discouraged by religious wars and hypocrisy, have a no less spiritual sense that promotes their seeing children with comparable compassion and concern. The more economic see children and their education in terms of productivity and competition with nations that score higher on standardized tests. Those who've known the mean and cold stare of poverty worry about economics, too, but from the children's vantage as individuals who need good educating to help them and their future children toward the better place they deserve. Political and social views, and basic values, much of that coming out of the where and how they grew up, can tint teachers' glasses as they look upon their students.

Their beliefs about children, how they develop and learn, must be relevant, too. Do teachers see a young child as incomplete or whole, as active or passive actors in life? Do they think it's all in the genes, blame or credit it all to the home, or are they moderates in the nature-nurture debate, believing that much of a child is both settled and malleable?

How rigid or flexible are their beliefs? When they hear that an incoming student is a bad apple, do they cringe, knowing for certain that he will ruin their school year? Or do they wait to see for themselves, leaving space for the child to convince them otherwise? Do they force their round pupils into square holes or can they alter their ideas about teaching or who a child is when experience tells them they should? Even in their early thirties are they old dogs who can't learn new tricks or, even in their sixties, young 'uns who never, for one minute, stop learning about children and education?

## CULTURE

The changing colors of our classrooms have compelled us to examine the effects of our culture on our teaching. My culture may differ from yours in the values we hold dear, the means we pursue to attain them, and the methods we use to instill them in our children. Some think the child is the center of the home and the universe, while others don't. Some think and plan for tomorrow, whereas others have good reasons for dwelling on the moment or hanging on to yesterday. We may differ in seemingly superficial ways, as in how we say hello, how we show respect, how we look or don't look in another's eyes, no less the eyes of an authority like the teacher. The boys-will-be-boys kind of noise, often taken for granted in the United States, is considered outrageous and troubled in some Asian homelands, while the reserved demeanor valued there is judged withdrawn and unassertive here. Not every culture praises the individualist every-person-for-himself credo. Our cultures and ethnic groups can disagree on virtually every aspect of life from the social to the intellectual, from how to ask a question to whether one can publicly cry or complain about bodily pain.

## HEALTH

How teachers feel can influence what they make of their teaching experience. Full of good health and pep, we can tolerate much more than when tired or flu-stricken. All but run over by overly hectic schedules, a good many of us drag ourselves about, day in, day out, perpetually lacking the rest our bodies cry for, never quite ready for the school day to begin. Tragically, prolonged or catastrophic illness can overwhelmingly unsettle our TeacherVision and how we work with our students, making those teachers who strive to cope and teach well in the face of such adversity heroes of the highest order. Those of us who are not teachers can only imagine what it must be like to enter the classroom with a headache.

## OTHERS' VIEWS AND OPINIONS

The TeacherVision of those around us can affect our own, confirming what we see or challenging us to think again. What other teachers and staff think about our students, and sometimes our teaching, can help us to see more clearly or lead us astray, depending on the clarity of their vision and our ability to have confidence in what we see while taking in whatever is worthwhile from them. Why do so many teachers and students, we can't help but ask ourselves, like and respect a student that we just can't stand? Our belief that what we see is *the* thing to be seen may not always be as true as we think.

These factors—knowledge, experience, beliefs, culture, health, and others' opinions—however hefty and influential as they may be, are not the only forces that tug and pull on teachers.

---

Who hasn't felt a gloomy depression darken the brightest of days? When we wake up happy and liking ourselves, even the cold rain feels like an old friend. Our *mood,* our current emotional state, colors all that we see and experience. It can be short-lived, as in our distemper at a roofer's having done a shoddy job or the joy following an old friend's phone call. Or it can be more enduring. Some greet life with a smile and a warm handshake, while others ever tow a rain cloud.

Consider a class of first graders who urge their teacher to take them on a planned walk to a nearby tidal pool. Eager to hunt starfish and shells, wanting to get out of school for a morning's romp, to them the sun appears to be breaking through the dense clouds, the rain letting up. But sitting in his seat at his desk, exhausted from a late night doing his overdue taxes, angry at something his wife said, angrier at something he said back, their teacher sees something else. As he peers out the same window, his squinting eyes swear the same gray sky grows darker. "It looks like it's going to be raining all morning," he says, craving for just one more hour of sleep. "We'll have to go another day."

Neither the teacher nor his class wants to deceive the other. They truly see what they see, viewing the same sky and world differently, through eyes as blurred by mood and motive, wishes and wish nots, as they are focused by physics and retinal physiology. It happens to all of us, all of the time.

---

Are our marriages good and satisfying, or are they troubled, leading us to seek from our students the intimacy and admiration we should get elsewhere, or distracting us with pain and loneliness? Do we get along with our own children, or are we ever scanning our classes for that special student who can make us feel less like a failed parent? How are our bank books—stable or depleting daily, our financial straits disrupting our sleep and preoccupying every worried minute of our lives, including those at school?

And how's our work going, our teaching? Do we feel well led by our principals, supported by our colleagues, and respected by the community? Are we satisfied having found our calling in life, or do we grow more sullen every year that we teach for a living, resenting how little money, prestige, and gratitude we get for all that we do? Do we own a deep sense of conviction that what we do is worthy, or have we long ago burned out, feeling that we do little good for anyone?

Teacher or not, our *life circumstances* profoundly affect us. These circumstances can be anguishing and enduring, as when we care for our own aging parents, torn between their needs and those of our own family, trying to meet the needs of our students all the while. We sometimes must come to work even when our own children need us, or when we are waiting for the results of a blood test or biopsy. Teachers courageously look into the eyes of other people's children even when they themselves are grief stricken over a miscarriage or being told they cannot have children of their own. From root canals to frightening estimates for auto repair, from the sadness over a pet put to sleep to the terror of having witnessed a violent crime, teachers must bear everything but the kitchen sink (unless the sink is leaking too). Every day teachers everywhere bravely come to school with such weighty matters on their minds, putting aside their own pain and dread just long enough to do what they must do. Unlike ditch diggers or certified public accounts, teachers can't easily escape their sorrows through their work, for in their work they see not deepening holes or rows of numbers, but boys and girls who continue to have wants and needs.

---

Wouldn't life be simpler if the factors that comprise TeacherVision exerted their powers in one predictable direction? But, as is no surprise, life and teachers don't work that way. The TeacherVision equation is one that defies reduction. It's not one part this, two parts that. It more resembles a stew that's been bubbling for some 20 to 60 years, a new and different ingredient added every second of those decades. To say that no two teachers' stockpots are alike is an understatement of colossal proportion. And quite frankly, even this metaphor fails to capture the complexity of TeacherVision, for human events and experience are infinitely varied in comparison to the relatively limited varieties of foods and spices.

But while the food chemist, even with her gas chromatograph, can neither decipher nor recreate our recipe, she can find out things about the stew. She can tell us some of what's in it, and how it's cooking and how it tastes now. She may be able to make suggestions as to what ingredients could improve it. And that is not unlike TeacherVision. We can never fully tease out all that goes into it. We can, however, come to see how it's doing, what's going into it, and what we can do to improve it.

---

On and on the list goes—from the gross to the sublime, from the hardly mattering to the abusive. All teachers—good and bad, some more, some less—chronically suffer such erratic sight. But, we must recall, our goal is not to do the impossible, ridding ourselves of every untoward feeling or sentiment. Rather, it is to better understand what we are about, and to ever work to teach well and comfortably with our human limitations and within ourselves.

# 6

# SPEAKING OF WORDS

*W*HAT IS THE POWER OF WORDS?
Ask the writers and poets who live their lives underground or exiled from the lands and people they love. Ask, if only we could, the less fortunate whose written words have brought torture and imprisonment. Ask the mothers and fathers, the husbands and wives, the sons and daughters, of protesters beaten and killed for doing nothing more than speaking out.

*What is the power of words?*
Ask the molested child who cannot testify to her own abuse out of fear of losing someone's love or under the threat of harm. Ask the immigrant or the senior citizen who, misunderstanding what he's told, loses his meager life savings in a scam. Ask all the men and women who've been unable to defend themselves against false accusations.

*What is the power of words?*
Ask the babies who rely on their mothers to read their wordless messages, to decipher whether they're craving her breast, a bottle, her caress, a nap, the babies who can only wail their hunger, writhe their colic, gurgle their wish to play, and yawn their sleepiness. Ask the mothers and fathers, too, who often can't tell a food cry from one asking to be warmed, dried, or entertained; the parents who try formula and lullabies, rocking and driving around the block one more time, going down the list of things that have once soothed their baby until something, until anything, works, or sometimes, too often, unable to stop the crying. Ask these parents, unable to figure out what their baby wants or needs, who pace their kitchens going nearly crazy out of the frustration they feel, each screech flaming the conviction that they are utter failures who should never have had children. Ask the children who can't keep up with the other kids' banter, who sit on the outside looking in.

*What is the power of words?* Though the writer, historian or psychologist may explain it more eloquently, no one knows the answer better than the person who has none.

---

*Hear ye. Hear ye. Hear all about it. Hear of the miracle of words, and the many things they can do for a child.*

While younger siblings can only grunt and point, our talkers can tell us precisely what cookie they want, *Not the vanilla ones, the Oreos;* why they cry, *'cause I miss Auntie;* and where it hurts, *the back of my throat.* But, more than just getting them the treats and attention they crave, language gives children a most basic tool to manage and make sense of their young, ofttimes confusing lives. They implore us, *Stay with me;* engage us, *help me;* amuse us, *I'm a little teacup;* and tell us how they really feel, *I don't want to go to school. I'm sad. I love you.*

Like a good friend, words allow children to not be so alone with what they feel, the worries and nightmares: *I'm mad. I'm scared. I dreamt a giant snake chased us and we all died;* and the joys and fantasies: *Chocolate is my favorite. I can't wait to see Mom tonight. I'm a princess.* Words foster their wondering and figuring out those around them. *Why are you screaming? How come I can't play with you? Jimmy's crying. Muffin's not hungry, he must be upset that Dad's not home yet.* Caught in a fight or some other trouble, they can tell their side of the story candidly as it is, personally edited to mute the blame and inflate the heroism, or by cunningly talking out both sides of their mouths.

Words confer a power that helps boys and girls to master the tasks of childhood that face them. Talking with their mother, for example, helps children come to see her as a separate person with her own separate inner thoughts and feelings and to bear the loss of a more physical connection with her. Likewise, being able to speak what they think and feel enables children to distinguish between their inner selves and the world at large. Giving words, and names, to their feelings further lays the seeds for a firm sense of reality and frees them to live less slavishly bound to the whims and pressures of their impulses. And their being able to protest aloud their having to grow up, ironically makes room for their doing so, for accepting their limitations and pursuing new independence and skills even as they scream and speak bloody murder to the contrary.

Their children's being able to comprehend words allows parents to prepare their sons and daughters for the dark and scary unknown of the future. A mother can warn her son that Daddy will pick him up from school tomorrow or that she'll be a bit late today. By telling her, a father can prepare his daughter for tomorrow's doctor's visit or next week's day camp. In times of misfortune, such as a loved one's death, the talking made possible by language helps children to express their fear and grief, and parents to appreciate and soothe that anguish.

And language offers not only diplomats and mediators but parents and children a means to negotiate around struggles. Limits can be declared or forewarned. Owning speech of their own, children can test these mandates and their parents' mettle by threatening, saying they will disobey, rather than by actually misbehaving. And if so inclined, parents can explain the reasons behind their rules and perhaps confirm the child's displeasure over them, this give and take serving as a foundation for future and satisfying parent and child discussions.

The using of words helps the child to grasp, process, understand, express, share, and cope with all she lives and experiences. These are just a beginning of the wonders that language, itself a wonder, can bring.

---

*Hate.*

Many teachers, like many parents—let's see, how can I put this delicately? Many teachers tend to disli . . . No, how about this? Many teachers favor language that is positive and . . . Not good. Let's try this: In my experience many teachers tend to sort of look rather disapprovingly . . . Who am I kidding? A fact's a fact. It's not to be argued. Many teachers *hate* that word, just plain hate it. But why? It's only a word, isn't it?

A professor of English I know doesn't like the word *hate* and thinks it's grossly overused. Not discriminating enough, he says. Better to use other words we have. Say, he suggests, that we're jealous, annoyed, disappointed, tired of . . . Hate rolls off the tongue too easily, he thinks. But articulate as he is and appreciating the subtlety and nuance of language as he does, he neglects a most basic point: the force of that word.

After 36 years of a good marriage and taking it black, don't you mean it when you tell him that you hate his still asking if you want cream with your coffee? And don't you mean it, too, when, unable to fit into the suit you bought just last year, you yell, "I hate this waistline"? We all hate the colds, the bills, the flat tires, the never-ending insults and trip-ups that life seems to enjoy dropping in our path. That well-spoken professor mistook the precision of language for its power. Sometimes, we need the ready hatchet of a word to grab the feeling—yes, the hatred—of the moment.

*I hate spelling. I hate German. I hate algebra.*

It's so negative, some teachers say. What have these subjects ever done to you? Nothing much, only made me do work some 180 nights or so a year, sit through classes that bore me or stress me or otherwise remind me of just how inept and hopeless I am. I know what it's like to misspell every other word I write, forget the simplest second grade fact and struggle with my own native language, English. It's easy to love something that comes easily, but I wouldn't know. And when you mis-hear a *hate you* in my *hate your subject,* that tells more about you than me and distracts you from my hurt and wound. (Though, frankly, what teacher doesn't take it personally?)

*I hate gym. I hate recess.*

Come on now, teachers may think. It's one thing to dislike difficult subjects, but to hate the fun times of the school day—what's that about?

I hate gym because I'm overweight and can barely run a yard with-out gasping and because I look disgusting in those ugly blue satin shorts they make us wear. I hate gym because I'm as coordinated as a 2-hour-old foal and don't particularly enjoy being laughed at every time I miss the ball or basket.

And I hate recess most because I am a social outcast and because I am unsafe on the playground. When you think all the children are play-ing so nicely, they are taunting me, calling me a girl, threatening to hurt me, especially if I tell anyone what they're doing to me. I prefer working in class, doing anything, any subject, for that's the time I don't worry for my life. You think hate is too strong a word. But if you knew what I know you'd agree that it's not strong enough to convey how miserable I feel, how awful life out there is for me.

*I hate you.*

To some these are the meanest, ugliest words of all. For most of us, they are the hardest to hear and to take. Some say hate is the flip side of love, of intense caring. Others can't see it's having anything to do with love, feeling only its deep sting and its seemingly total rejection of them and who they are. Some of us react with sadness and a wish to know why and to undo it, to restore the love lost inside it. Others, too hurt, too wounded, too angry, hate back, giving our haters what we think they deserve. How much easier it is to accept and confirm others' love for us than their disfavor, their disappointment, maybe even the hatred they feel for us at times. So many of the most necessary parts of life are the hardest. And who among us doesn't hate that?

---

Sticks and stones may break our bones. But what about names? When I was a child I was pretty certain that they could never hurt me. But today everything has been turned upside down, or more aptly, knocked or kicked there.

Today, and for sadly good reason, a child who voices his dislike for a teacher or another child is not given much sympathy or ear. In today's understandable climate of no tolerance—meaning no hate or violent speech allowed—that child will be rushed off to the principal, where his parents and perhaps the police will be notified. The *I'm gonna get you* shouted innocently around the playground when I was a boy has grown into something hideous and fearsome. Real children packing and even using real weapons have taught us the hard lesson that some people mean what they say, even when what they say is a promise to hurt someone. This new order of random violence has created a thorny dilemma of the highest order and most profound implication, and one befuddling what we know to be true.

Once upon a time, and still for the majority, children could tell fact from fantasy, thought from action. For them the connection, and distinction, between word and deed was a clear one that grew more solid and reliable every day. For these children, really most children, language became a way to help manage what they thought and felt. *I feel mad enough to hit you* but instead I will tell you about that wish in words. *I could kill you,* but not really.

For most children, the powerful weapon of language strengthens their self-control. Screaming at us or telling us they can't stand us and feel hurt by what we said about them offers an alternative to raging physical acts and silent withholding. Language allows children to put the energy and substance of their impulses into words, words that, though physically harmless, can actually convey all of what they feel. Children's words are a way station between thoughts and actions along the road toward a civilized self.

The power to speak aids them in moments of their greatest frustration. *I quit. I can't take it anymore. Shut up!* Who of us doesn't yell profanity or at least something when hammering a thumb? In fact, isn't it exactly those times for which our choicest and most strongly felt words were made?

Consider a girl who was fully out of control, kicking and hitting any sibling, parent, classmate, or teacher that got in her way, her kindergarten close to giving up on her. Desperate, her parents brought their daughter to me. "This may be hard," I told them, "for you, not just Terry." Whatever it takes, they said. And they did do whatever it took—being firmer, being kinder (for they often said mean things to Terry), and being more aware of themselves (for they often took their own upsets out on her)—until, that is, her father called one day. "Thanks for all you've done. We've decided that tomorrow's session will be Terry's last."

I was taken aback, for Terry had done well. Her aggression had stopped and the school, no longer feeling unsafe, had a chance to see and like the curious and engaging child they'd gotten to know. Neither Terry nor her parents had seemed anything but delighted with our shared work. Only at her last hour, and at my inviting her father in, did I hear the impetus to his sudden decision.

One night at the dinner table Terry had told her parents that she hated them and wished she had other parents. "I'm not bringing her here so she can talk to me like that," her father said, his anger feebly hiding his hurt. "If she's going to talk like that she can just start kicking again for all I care."

But, loud words and all, Terry's father did care. A moment of my listening to the pain over his child's words was enough to free his thinking. Terry, he came to see, had spoken because she was feeling better about her relationship with her parents. They, she believed, would now want to hear what she felt. Her father admitted, too, that much of his daughter's problem probably stemmed from his own temper and ways he'd been rough with her. Terry's therapy resumed and she thrived.

Her teachers took the bumps in Terry's growth in stride. They recognized that her speaking out was a good sign. Her mean and angry words enabled her to not do mean and angry things. And soon enough, the mean words stopped. Over time, and not too long a time, good words came more. For Terry enjoyed being a good girl whom peers and teachers liked.

Realistically, teachers and schools can't be as tolerant and patient as a therapist in his cozy office. They cannot stand idly by as a child rants, berates, or threatens. But what can they do, short of calling the F.B.I., casting the child out, or calling in parents, who might not be helpful?

When hearing *He's an idiot* called out in their class, some teachers will see a black-and-white scene of victim and his perpetrator, the name-caller deserving nothing but a severe squelching and rebuke. But other teachers might view a more complex scene and an opportunity to discuss the matter for the benefit of everyone, including the screamed-at child, who has to cope with teasing even when out of the teacher's protective sight; the name-caller himself, struggling with a learning problem he's ashamed of; the class, who relate to both sides of the issue; and, themselves, the teachers who want to make their own views known and wish to show that neither words nor heated debate frightens them.

These teachers recognize further that children who curse and speak the angriest often fear, hate, and distrust a less notorious class of four-letter words. Unable to stand what they *feel,* they are strangers to *love,* rejecters of the *help* they crave and need, acting as if they could *care less* about the shambles their lives are in, holding no *hope* for themselves and their futures.

In the end, if what we hear in the news is accurate, names can eventually lead to broken bones and worse. So we try our best to bring awareness where we can, change children when we can, and stop dangerously hateful and hurtful speech when we can't do either, trying to see the humanity, however shamed and shrunken, the feeling that hides beneath the seemingly unfeeling façade and rhetoric.

———————

*What do you call a green parakeet, a rotten peach, and a pair of socks between two slices of bread? A sandwich. Why didn't the cow go dancing? She wasn't in the mooooood. What did the doe say to her baby? You're such a little deer. Attila the Nun, Alexander the Grape, a Benny saved is a Benny urned.*

It's not by accident that children like such jokes. And it's not by accident that thousands of miles apart, in the country and the city, so many of us, and so many of our students, hear and laugh at the same jokes, even as we put them down as lame. Punsters and silly poets extraordinaire abound in our classrooms, finding delight at every double meaning and misspoken word. However strange it might seem to the adults, these children know that words can be hugged, embraced, beat up, twisted, and spit—even more than can their old and trusty teddy bears and blankets. But unlike those cuddlies, children can bring their words wherever they go, even to their classrooms.

And, as every teacher knows, the reading that follows on the heels of language can also bring pleasure and comfort. Some children's love of books is unbounded, books being the place they go for entertainment and consoling, for facts and reassurance. Books offer information on every aspect of life and nature, including fine literature that understands children's feelings and their struggles. And books can be good friends in a deeper sense, in the way that they become bedtime companions, comforting stand-ins for the parents who sleep in a separate room or when a child at school misses home.

Recognizing the power of language, wanting her students to care deeply for words, a teacher listens slowly, allowing herself and class to stop and smell the words, as it were, taking the time to note the clever, if distracting, play on words that the wise guy, the kid who supposedly hates language arts, offers up. Subtly but with deliberate intent, the teacher nurtures the growth of a class culture and language that, though sounding much like English, only they share.

It's a private language that invites ingenuity, playfulness, and involvement. The *but we just read yesterday* that one boy spoke with a grin becomes the class's yearlong shorthand for anything that any student doesn't feel like doing, becoming, too, a nice way for students to express their protests even as they cooperatively pull out their books. The teacher's own *Have I got a treat for you, guys* becomes their idiomatic phrase, and a smoothing one at that, for some unavoidable task she knows they'll hate doing. And a guest speaker's referring to World War One and *World War Woo* becomes the cliché of choice whenever any of them grow tongue-tied or trip over a word.

Like a good children's writer, this teacher lets her love of words show. She speaks so that the children can understand what she says, but she isn't shy to test-fly new and intriguing words. She enjoys not only what the witty children say, but also what the quieter or not so glib talkers strain to express. She rules a land in which all can speak safely and has plenty of time to wait for the slower to speak their minds. *I don't know* or that same old shrug of the shoulders can't deter her. *What are you thinking? Take your time, we want to hear what you thought of the story. You saw a skunk in your yard? Tell us more.*

And she takes care what she says to them. We won't hear *Sit down and shut up* here, though her class is as well mannered as any. Respectful speech leads the way, assuming the best. But when more is needed, when her class or a student dares her, she still speaks with a clear and generous spirit. She makes perfectly clear what she wants heard without ridicule. *I have all the words I have for good reason, and I will use them. And I expect you'll use yours, too.* She instructs the best way, by showing, not telling, her pupils day in, day out. Word in, word out.

---

We've learned the hard way. We can no longer allow students to attack others with hate or, themselves, grow hateful from mistreatment. And yet, to dismiss, reject, or punish our students' words too readily carries its own risks. People, and that means children and teachers, too, say what they say for good reason. To steamroll over those reasons can lead us and our students to bad places. Nor can we afford to take our own words any less seriously. If, in a classroom economy that is robust and delicate, words are the currency, we and our students need to learn to manage our money, our *what we say,* responsibly.

# 7

# SEX MATTERS

A CHAPTER ON SEX? Where did this come from? We're reading about good and wholesome things like children, teachers, and their classrooms, and whack, like a flower pot fallen from some third-floor balcony, a chapter on sex falls smack on our heads.

All of us, our children and students included, marinate in a world of sex. But it's different than it was when we were kids, a lot different. Today's children can find it, whether the real or virtual kind, more easily than they can a pack of cigarettes. Teenage boys and girls, still essentially children, coolly discuss acts their parents, red-faced, can barely imagine. Some loving parents, sadly resigned to their children's promiscuity, hope only that their children practice safe sex or that they be lucky enough to get through their experimenting without the mishap and mayhem of unwanted pregnancy and AIDS. And even the children who aren't looking for sex meet up with it as they watch movies and television shows allegedly rated for them or overhear wilder classmates fantasize and brag, and even as they try earnestly to research a school project on the Internet, their typing in the keywords *ocean* and *picture* taking them to *XXX* sites featuring tanned women cavorting on California beaches.

However offensive to some, it's indisputable that children think about sex. But that doesn't mean they benefit from getting or even seeing what they think about, and we can be sure that what's out there can outdo any child's imagining. We don't need child psychologists or the clergy to tell us that seeing or, worse, experiencing too much too soon can harm children. Yet, as we joke about iron-clad chastity belts or, better yet, glass bubbles in which to preserve our children, in truth, shielding them from our culture is somewhat like trying to plug a dam's worth of leaks with two thumbs.

It's in this unfortunate context that we meet our students. At this juncture—in the class and in this chapter—teachers who just won't hear of it, who don't believe in childhood sexuality or who find it too wrong, too overwhelming, or too disheartening can look the other way. But they, like ostriches in the sand, will be avoiding what's there, and in doing so will miss golden opportunities to understand and help their students, not just in terms of the down and dirty, but in the subtler forms that children's sexuality assumes in even the youngest pupils.

---

Oh, that Freud had a dirty mind, didn't he? All that talk about sex. And not just in adults or even adolescents. He dared to suggest that the concept of sexuality held relevance, big relevance, for children, too, even young ones. But Freud's conception of childhood sexuality may not be quite what we think.

To understand his view we must go back to the beginning, to the babies who are well fed, nursed and nurtured by their mothers. Not unlike our puppies who experience much of their world by biting, licking, and chewing it, babies explore the world mouth first. Taking in mommy and her milk, or its bottle, or that yummy peach mush, our babies yield to the wondrous pleasure of rich liquids and soft compotes that warm their wiggling, irritable bodies and satisfy their hunger. Let our babies play with our key chain and, even more than studying it with their eyes and fingers, they'll stick it in their mouths. Hold our dear babies to our face, their sweet searching mouths will open like so many giant Os eating our nose. No mother needs a Viennese psychoanalyst to point out the bodily joy and comfort her baby experiences orally.

That same mother may have a harder time recognizing the later pleasure her growing baby takes in its bowel movements and urinating, especially as her job of cleaning it up tends to be anything but a party. Letting it go anywhere and anytime, exactly in the instant when nature calls— what a delight. No waiting for a meeting to end, the bell to ring, or another agonizing 11 miles to the next turnpike rest area. And afterward, bodies relieved, their loving parents clean the mess, washing, patting, and powdering, showering them with love and kisses all the while. Learning to control their pooping and peeing, in itself, can be pleasing too. No less than with adult sex, holding it in and letting it go, tightening the muscles that guard their sphincters and relaxing them, heightening the tension and releasing it, all can in itself feel good as well as bring a more grownup satisfaction of controlling their own bodies.

To no one's astonishment, this bodily focus eventually comes to include the little boy's penis and the little girl's vagina. Constant fiddling and touching, hands ever mindlessly migrating southward, contorting pelvises this way and that, making a slide of daddy's legs, squeezing back hard against mommy's hug, doing whatever it takes to make contact in that area, particularly with those they most love. And why wouldn't they?

For the first 5 years of their lives, many children have been adored in the deep-as-the-ocean high-as-the-sky ways that poets and songwriters usually devote to the grandest and most passionate of lovers. How could these boys and girls not take erotic pleasure of the most profound kind from the tender caresses, consoling hugs, giggling belly farts, luxurious bubble baths, and thrilling horseplay they know at the hands of their truest loves of all—their parents? That is what can happen when all works as it should, or at least, as we hope. That is healthy.

But for all of this indulgence and doting there is much frustration, too. Over the noise of their cries, claims of monsters-in-residence and tip-toeing footsteps, we calmly teach them to sleep in their own beds, occasionally banning them from our rooms out of our own need for private respite or pleasure. Though they may like rubbing against us like some scratching pole, we gently distract them just as we guide and manage their erotic wishes for us, wishes that occasionally get out of hand with their, for example, trying to climb in our nightclothes, or affection that evolves into its sometimes close cousin, aggression. Recognizing that the wishes they hold around their bodies are as healthy and precious as they are common and natural, we neither seductively exploit them nor coldly punish them. By gently helping children manage themselves, we encourage the sublimating, the channeling of that love into broader and safer interests.

"Wow, you're body is growing," offered by a mother to her toddler proudly showing off his penis, even as she gently helps him back into his pants, allows him to feel good, and without shame, about his excitement that he is growing into a big boy. A father's sympathetic smile or "What a wonderful dream" to the little girl who shares her wish to marry him, even as he walks her back to her own bedroom, allows her to relish in her ever-growing more and more like her mother. At its best, our compassionate response to our children's wish that we cuddle, stroke, care for, and admire their growing bodies gives them enough of what they seek to ease the bittersweet sting that the giving up of growing up inflicts.

When given understanding but not allowed to run amok, children's strong thoughts and feelings about their young version of sex can go productively underground to find gratification elsewhere. A curiosity about their own and their parents' bodies can evolve into a love of science and a drive to know the insides of insects, clocks, or the human psyche. A wish to have their growing bodies seen and praised by their parents can contribute to a love of the stage, a gymnastic poise, or a calling to leadership, to be up front. And the experience of having been well-loved and cherished can foster children's own tender spirit toward the world and others, inspiring their own fantasies of being a good parent or even a teacher when they grow up.

In one of the ironies that so frequently describe human existence, it's precisely the kind of childhood sexuality I've been talking about that should worry us least. For the children who've been well-loved and cared for, the ones who've had their feelings understood, accepted, and guided, the ones who've been disciplined as they should be, are the ones who generally come to school most ready to be students and to learn. It's the too many others—those who've been exploited, overstimulated, or neglected—who are most at the whim of their impulses, most distracted by their body and its needs, most at risk for sex-related problems, and most burdened by earlier pieces of childhood that have yet to be put in their proper place.[1]

---

Mrs. Bowdoin wondered if her cheeks were as fiery red as they felt. A calm teacher with a well-earned reputation for unflappability, she was as embarrassed as she could remember feeling. Nor could she believe what she'd heard. Though she'd later have a good laugh about the darnedest things kids say, in the heat of the moment she felt shocked, frazzled, and at a loss for words.

*Do you and your husband make babies?*

"We don't talk like that in here!" Mrs. Bowdoin barked, not her typical style. "And I don't want to hear such talk again or I'll have to call your parents." The little girl got it. She put her head on the desk and said nothing for the rest of the day.

As it turned out, Mrs. Bowdoin didn't have to call the parents, for that night the girl's mother called her to complain. "What," she asked, "was so terrible? She's only 8 years old. Aren't elementary school teachers supposed to handle things like this? They're just children."

While it wasn't every day that one of her second graders asked such a question, it wasn't once in a blue moon either. In fact, other children had asked questions about sex and making babies, some much bolder. Nor was this the only time a child had pointed the spotlight on her relationship with her husband. Why am I so upset now, she wondered to herself, agreeing with everything the mother said.

It all came clear while she was driving home and stopping to buy a bottle of wine for a special dinner she'd planned that night. Bravely that morning, and for the first time ever, she'd directly brought up sex with her husband. "Why aren't you more interested?" To her amazement, her keep-everything-to-himself husband answered her. He told her about mounting stress at work, opening a heartfelt talk and closeness that buoyed and excited both of them. Like a Patriot missile, her curious pupil's comment had zoomed right to the core of the just woken intimacy and romance on her mind and threatened to expose the joy so close to the surface.

The next day Mrs. Bowdoin returned to school as rock solid and self-contained as ever. She made peace with her student and reassured the class that they could always ask questions, though it didn't mean she'd always answer them the way they'd like.

How can our own attitudes and views about sex, others' and our own, not impact our teaching? Those of us with hang-ups around our own bodies may frown upon the ease and dare that our more liberated students display, saving our praise for more inhibited children. Women who understandably resent a male-dominated society may hold more respect for the assertive tomboy (and her mother) than for the equally independent girl (and *her* mother) who happens to like flowery dresses and making pretty things. Homophobic men may treat less manly students as second-class citizens or keep all their male students at a cold arms' length. How satisfied are we in our marriages and relationships? Do we come to school feeling loved and secure, or do we cross the threshold needing love, attention, and—maybe—sex? Every aspect of our own sexuality and relationship to our own bodies and selves bears impact on our work in the classroom. The more we understand ourselves, the more likely it is that we'll use our teaching in the child's best interest, and not to meet our needs or mollify our hurts. And if we can refresh our minds as to all that sex really means, we'll come to school better equipped to understand our students' words and gestures, even when they provoke or perturb our own currents.

———————

Squirming kids. Jittery kids. Kids who can't stay put in a chair for a second. What do these kids have to do with sex?

These kids are children who, for all kinds of reasons—the way they were born, the way they were raised—have bodies that are ever in a state of tension that can't be quieted. However much it might please us and their parents, these children just can't sit still. Their moving isn't meant to bug us; it aims to make them feel less uncomfortable.

Their bodies, many children have described, feel the way other people's do in those rare nights, for example, when despite our utter fatigue and need for sleep, our legs itch with energy for a walk or a run. Not moving, described one such boy, hurts him. Built better for a hunting-and-gathering society and an active outdoor life, these children are disadvantaged in a contemporary world that rewards, if not demands, a capacity to sit behind a desk or at a keyboard for hours.

What's wrong with our doing anything benign that can help to settle a child into his work and our class, even teenagers whose bodies pulse with feelings and anxieties enough to electrify the dullest lead pencil? Why can't children's experience of what they feel, and what works for them, be valued and inform what transpires in the classroom? Why can't we listen to what their bodies and they try to tell us?

These children put us in a frustrating bind. Recognizing that they lack the innate capacity to quell their own arms and legs, we give them some room to fidget, particularly if they are pleasant, cooperative, and learning. When they say, and demonstrate, that they can listen better to the lesson when braiding their hair or building paper clip chains, we believe them. For every boy who needs silence to study we know there really is a second who has an equal and opposing need for music in the background. And we can even appreciate that a little thing like chewing gum might help keep a restless child on task and in her seat. Unfortunately, to allow for unlimited moving about, background noise, and gum, for example, would distract a majority of the children and cause other problems that we know well enough. Teaching in a democracy, we are eventually pulled in by the commonweal, that which on the average is the best for everyone. And so we do what we can, sometimes bending, looking the other way, instituting a novel approach. Though we can't always slow our students' wiggling, we can appreciate what it must be like and try not to take it personally. It can be much harder to accept a child's constant movement when that child is aggressive, disruptive, dishonest, and not learning. Unfortunate, but true.

---

Puberty? What is it about that word that makes teens, and some parents, giggle in a way that the term *adolescence* doesn't? Because of its sounding like *pubic*, I suspect. *Sex is coming*, I imagine, it's heard. *Look out. Here it comes.* Like a grinning little creature—part innocent child, part salivating satyr—*puberty* seems to capture the neither-here-nor-there and the bothness of the early, now called tween, years.

What a wrench this puberty throws into the works of children, as if growing up isn't hard enough. Now, on top of every other thing they contend with, they have to feel their bodies heating up and doing all sorts of things they aren't used to. So much of the time they still feel like little kids who want to sit on their parents' laps, and yet, with every music video that passes, they are looking, sounding, and even smelling more like adults.

I could describe the cataclysmic flux, the tumult, the sudden pulsing that strains the adolescent body, but colorful and vivid as my portrayal might be, it would fail to capture the unsettling power of adolescence on children's psyche and their view of themselves. The changes their bodies undergo challenge much of what they know about themselves. Becoming sexual is a confusing business, most of all for children who have yet to think of themselves as sexual. It can tongue-tie the boy who—self-conscious of his feeble beard, his cracking voice, and his own strange odor—just yesterday could easily talk to the girls in his class. It can sadden the girl who—her breasts developing, it being that time of the month—just yesterday, it seems, could wrestle unabashedly with her father and brothers. *Am I getting or losing?* might well be teens' anthem.

And once again, just as we appear to be seeing sex as sex—petting, kissing, and all the bases—we are reminded of its less sexy meanings. Not, mind you, in the tentative hand-holding we see between the boys and girls who we know will go slow. No, we can see the less sexy meanings much more clearly in the wild ones, the seventh graders who already have done it all, perhaps with more than a few. These children, we fear, missed out on early experiences that made them love and care for themselves. These children, doing it wildly and impulsively, can spout invincibility. *We won't get pregnant. We won't get AIDS.* But we don't have to look very deep to see the vulnerability. *We are not worth caring about,* their unprotected sex proclaims. *We are not worth keeping safe,* their going off with complete strangers or those who mistreat them mumbles.

How can we help these children to manage their newfound sexuality and minimize its messing up their education? The same steady and thoughtful (and plodding along doing the best we can) way we help them to see, comprehend, and cope with everything else. Just the same way.

----

Snips and snails and puppy dog tails. What the heck is a snip anyway? And how come girls don't got any? This is just one of the questions that modern science has asked when analyzing the composition of our children.

And, of course, we all know what girls are made of. Even the ones who are thieves and murderers and double spies are sugar and spice, and all that good stuff. Somehow, so are the many girls in third grades across the country who daily devastate their weaker classmates with baleful gossip and humiliating rejection.

Well, it's time the truth be told. Some girls are full of puppy tails and there are some boys who are everything nice, even some boys who run fast and shoot hard. There are boys whose chemical makeup looks nothing like that of the boys beside them, and there are girls and boys whose ingredients are identical save a $Y$-chromosome and a couple of minor genes.

I'm not saying that boys aren't from Mars or that girls aren't from Venus. And, in fact, I mean that. Boys often do differ from girls, just as girls do from boys. For all my own time on the analytic couch, and my work in this area, I'm still the guy that stand-up comics self-disparagingly mock, the ones who are prone to ever fixing things, decimating clean kitchens and reacting in such predictable ways to my wife's equally ladylike behaviors (or at least, what the comediennes define as such).

What does my nonsense mean to say? Gender bias is real—in every direction. Growing up I had teachers who preferred the boys, and teachers who were prejudiced against us. It made a difference. Countless studies have shown that girls traditionally have been called on less, graded less well, challenged less, and expected less to excel, especially in science, math, and the many other subjects somehow assumed to be Man's own, deterring not only their education but the evolution of their authentic selves.

Much has since been made of this partiality. But how much has really changed? The pattern can be subtle and enduring. Look around and listen up. Whom do we invite to the board and encourage with our ahems and tell us more? Whom do we see as our young Einsteins and Pasteurs? Do we give up too easily on the girls, or perhaps the boys, investing more in one over the other?

Look deeper and listen closely. Do we prefer one gender over the other? Or do we view one as more likable and appealing, judging the second sex, nonetheless, as more academically competent, promising, or interested? What are our beliefs about boys and girls in general and specific, begging the significance of what we believe about grown men and women?

Should we find biases, or even franker prejudices, what then? We can turn away and go on as before, none the wiser. But, noting what is and what we do, even if we don't enjoy what we see, we can change the way we go about our work. Or we can go all the way, taking these steps as just the beginning of a new and expanded vision, a stimulus to our questioning all that we see and do in the classroom.

Likely no one is ever going to turn us in for having a bit of preference. But we know who we are. And whatever we do, the choice is our own. Won't it be nice, however, when our daughters and female students can tell us, in the most scientific terms, exactly what girls, boys, and as yet undiscovered planets are made of, while our sons cry over the unfairness of this new equality—not because they have to, but because they want to?

———————

Sexual harassment and the school. I tried to write a smooth transition for this subject, one that softens its abruptness. But I couldn't. The matter isn't wanted here, in this chapter and book, just as it's unwanted and has no place in our schools, or anywhere. And so, however unpleasant and derailing, we must face it.

Forgetting the occasional ape man, I suppose, whose chromosomes demands it, for the most part sexual harassers are made not born. Noble teachers can attempt their best to rehabilitate a young provocateur, just as therapists can do their best to help him explore his need to torment others. But that is another story. In the classroom, in the hallways, and on the playground, these children need, more than anything, to be stopped. No child deserves to be called *faggot* or be otherwise humiliated with sexual put-downs or propositions. If the escalating tragedies in our schools teach us anything, it's the danger of a child's day after day suffering the taunts and rejection of peers. Who of us is so secure we can show up for work weeks and months and years on end, our co-workers regularly accusing us of being queer or saying precisely what they know will most shame us in front of everyone? It's true that victims can occasionally ask for what they get but that never justifies the sexual predator or bully.

And so, we take even little instances of harassing seriously, halting it, making sure that the child understands why we won't tolerate it. For the basically well-intentioned children our disapproval and a talk might be enough. Some will require firm consequences, and yet others, those, we fear, headed to be adult abusers, will need even sterner punishments and our engaging their parents in the solution.

From little harassers grow big ones.

———————

Sex matters in all sorts of ways. But, if we think only of the *X*-rated kind, we'll miss the *R, PG,* and even, *G*-rated varieties that are much more important, pervasive, and influential in the lives of our students in and out of the classroom.

## NOTE

1. But not always, of course. Due to overriding biology, neurology, and temperament some children experience difficulty in school in spite of the best parenting. And there are plenty of exceptions in the opposite direction, too. Some children from the bleakest of beginnings make dedicated and successful pupils.

# 8

# WHO'S TENDING THE MELTING POT?

LOOK AT ALL THE CHILDREN, the all so different from each other children. Enormous smiles full of gleaming teeth. Each child holding the hand of the next one, 1,436 children forming a snail-shaped spiral, hand in hand in hand. Chinese, Kenyan, Australian, English, Pakistani, Canadian, Swedish, Ukrainian, Syrian, Nigerian, Guatemalan, Spanish, Israeli, Tibetan, and every nationality, each child carrying its nation's flag and wearing its traditional dress. They sing, too, about love and peace, and about having to take care of a planet that more than 6 billion people share. What a lovely and heartwarming scene, even if on television, staged for an Olympic opening ceremony; even if it is not quite real.

Being children, they notice how different they all are. Not in a bad or discriminating way. In the way we admire the varieties of flowers and butterflies. Skins of so many colors and tones. Faces shaped this way and that, with hair and eyes to match. The children love what they see. It neither frightens nor repels them.

But the children's parents. That is a different story. They're not always so happy with what they see. Some of them watch from prisons where they are political prisoners; others watch from countries other than their own to which they've fled from persecution or intolerable hardship; and, yet others, much too poor to own a television, listen to the majestic fanfare on the radio while only imagining the splendor. If we understood their culture's gestures and idioms, we'd see that they scoff, blessing the children's innocence but knowing its frailty, pushing away the image of these children in their own prison garb or the uniform of menial labor. Even some parents who live under less oppressive governments shake their heads. All the colors of the rainbow locked arm in arm, heart to heart. The fluff of corporate advertising, they think, having nothing to do with the hate, anger, and injustice that really portray their world, and that they battle daily and only wish they could shelter their children from.

Other parents are disgusted by this celebration of life and people. Seeing black children mix with white sickens them. It's evil, they believe, and unnatural. God intended for peoples to be apart. They want to shut the television off but leave it on so they can vent their poisonous hate, screaming cruel and prejudiced remarks aloud at the children who don't look like them.

America may be a melting pot but it isn't any vegetable soup in which all the ingredients came from old Mr. McGregor's garden. Many ran for their lives from other countries, fleeing religious persecution, political oppression, racial or ethnic cleansing, and starvation. Others came against their will, on slave ships. And then thousands more got here by careful planning, determined to find a better life for their families, some with pockets full of money, some with no more than the clothes on their backs. Africans, Germans, Russians, Indians, Japanese, Lithuanian, and Lebanese. All so different, each as unique as the most one-of-a-kind snowflake, and all so much the same, all wanting the best for themselves but, more so, wanting the best for their children. Open-minded or bigoted, these people wanted their children to have every opportunity. And that, they knew, meant some kind of education. Though they may not have wanted their children to go on the same bus or be in the same classroom with mine, most agreed that they wanted their children somehow schooled.

---

Few immigrants have had an easy life, most toiling long and hard for small, uncertain, and slow-coming rewards. But certain groups, foremost African-Americans, have had it worse. In the cruelest of crimes against humankind, these people were simply stolen away from their families and villages, and shackled to wooden boats that they themselves rowed across the ocean. No words can bring to life what that trip must have been like in all its gruesome horror: the confinement in the ship's bowels, the bodies pushed beyond human limits, the whippings, the beatings. But that wasn't the worst of it. Those poor men, treated less kindly than the most hated dogs, endured their abuse, not buoyed by the immigrant's dream of the new world he'd find soon for his family, but knowing that they would never see their loved ones, their wives and children, their mothers and fathers, and their homelands ever again.

Today's African-American children, and certain other peoples of color, thank goodness, are neither kidnapped and sold nor paddling slave ships and lugging cotton bales. But these children carry stone-heavy loads of their own, loads their more fortunate peers are spared.

Consider a hypothetical third grader, Scott Forman, an African-American boy who lives in an apartment in Boston's inner city. By his first year of school he'd already witnessed a man beaten in daylight on his block; knew a man, his best friend's uncle, who was killed, and is pretty sure something real bad has happened to his teenage cousin. He isn't sure what happened exactly but he saw her and his aunts crying and upset, and heard his parents yelling at his own sister to be real careful and not go out alone.

Though Scott's parents are good and upstanding people, they've been able to do little to change the tough neighborhood in which they live. Drug dealers and hoodlums rule the street, making the ballparks and basketball courts less than the happy places they should be. On many occasions Scott's father has wanted to go out and take matters into his own hands, but his wife, Scott's mother, dissuaded him, knowing there were punks who'd think nothing of hurting her honest and kindly husband.

As do many urban children, especially African-American, Scott has asthma. Whether due, as some speculate, to the irritation of polluted city air, allergic reaction to the cockroaches that assail city apartment buildings, or the erratic heat that runs too cold and too hot, Scott's breathing has been bad lately. Having to run out in the middle of the night, taking cabs they can ill afford, hanging around a city hospital emergency room till the wee hours of the morning, doesn't help either. Lacking good enough health insurance, they don't have the luxury of a pediatric practice down the street to treat Scott before his attacks flare.

Having missed many days of school due to his respiratory problems, Scott is falling behind. This has distressed his hard-working father, a 49-year-old man who works in a nursing home laundry. He sorely wants Scott to do well in school so that he can have a good home in a safe place with money enough to buy a car, a doctor's care, and maybe even all the treats and vacations he wishes he could give to Scott and the family. Though as motivated to succeed in school as his father could hope, Scott has mild dyslexia and is somewhat disorganized. Unlike the parents of his peers in the more affluent suburbs, however, his parents can't afford to buy him private lessons with reading specialists and tutors; and his school, strained by lack of resources and overwhelming need, can only do its inadequate best. But Scott, as decent and compassionate as any boy could be, doesn't complain. He feels lucky to have good parents and a good home. He'd be the first one to tell us of friends who have less, don't have two parents or good ones, live on even harsher blocks, and aren't as smart as he.

But poverty and its lethal fallout are not Scott's only stress. He also lives in a racist society. Many nights he's heard his father and uncles discuss politics and civil rights and the way America has mistreated their people. Newspaper headlines and the television news—black man dragged to his death behind a pick-up truck, racial tensions in America's high schools—don't get by without his noticing. And he has his own personal experiences with racism. Children at a summer camp egged him on to "rap like a nigger." When taking him and a friend to a movie downtown, his sister was pushed around and called horrible names by teenagers who seemed to own the sidewalk. And the injury that hurts and enrages him most is the scar on his pretty and favorite aunt's forehead, a gash cut by a rock some white grownup threw at her years ago for a sin no greater than riding a court-ordered bus to an elementary school in another part of town.

Just a boy, with a boy's shoulders and back, Scott bears the weight of poverty and of prejudice, even as he copes with all of the other, everyday tasks that face all children, whatever their color. The psychologies of attachment and separation, of toilet training and independence, of sexual and intellectual development, all apply as much to Scott as to every other child. So does the psychology of identity, though for Scott it is so much more complex and arduous. How confusing to grow into himself when so much of the world and his experience tries to tell him that people of his color are not as good, are worth less, or at least will face a life so much harder. Like all children of color, having their own stories and burdens, Scott has extra courage, heart, and resilience. He has to.

───────────

Several years ago a graduate school friend and I took my son to the Children's Museum. While my son explored a three-dimensional model of an ear as big as his head, I was drawn to the life-size Native American village. I walked about the teepee, studying and admiring its architecture until, noticing my young son looking over, I made a loud whooping sound the way Hollywood Indians did when attacking Fort Apache. A security guard quickly came over and pointed me to a plaque posted at the rear of the display. In bold letters it specifically asked that visitors refrain from making war cries. Rightly chastised, I slipped over to join my son at the giant ear, where I told him what happened. "I could have told you that," he said assuredly. "It's like making fun of them." I walked off with him and my friend, a great deal embarrassed, and noticing, then and as the day passed, that it was the parents, not children, who did their pathetic rain dances.

Am I racist? I know enough about me to say I've laughed at jokes I shouldn't have and that I've thought things I felt ashamed of. Under stress I've automatically jumped to conclusions based on nothing more than stereotype. In truth, I admit I've even told jokes that poke fun at ethnic and racial groups, my own and others. Whooping it up in that teepee reminded me that I am far from a perfect specimen of humanity (despite my long respect for Native American values, especially toward the earth and nature). I know for sure that if I were a Native American, and had been standing nearby with my son, watching the grown white man hop and hoot, however foolish, would have angered and saddened me. It would have told me what I probably already suspected: that we are seen and treated as different. I also would have thought me racist.

As teachers, seeing where we stand is a good thing. Knowing and admitting our blind spots to ourselves can allow us to remedy them, if we choose. Merely announcing them as ours, however—*hey, I'm just a cheap bastard; so I say mean things, that's who I am*—is not a blank check to keep on keeping our bad ways. If we wish to be less racist and prejudiced, we'll need to do some honest looking in the mirror and probably more.

We'll do this because, we hope, we want to teach our students better and we recognize that our misperceptions get in the way. Throwing international food festivals or singing a Kwanzaa song at the fifth-grade holiday chorus may be nice, and may make us feel good about ourselves and our school. But, we must ask candidly, does that really change who we are? Does that make us more understanding of our students or are we gesturing?

Do we realize what it's like to be different, we must first wonder. Do we know what it feels like to be ostracized because of the color of our skin or the language that we speak? Teachers of color know it well. The rest of us probably don't, even though we think we do.

What beliefs, we further probe, do we hold about this group or that? Do we think some are smarter, better, or more worth our educating? Do we hold one cultural background in higher esteem than others? Do we assume that some kind of parents love their children more? Do we expect every student and parent to value education exactly as we do? Yes answers are worth 5 points, and as you can guess, the higher the score, the more worrisome our vision and teaching.

If we falsely believe certain children to be less earnest about school, we risk not pushing them as hard as we should. Should we not understand another's social customs, we might misread a respectful lack of eye contact to be rude or avoidant. Believing the individual reigns supreme, we are sure to arrogantly devalue cultures that hold greater faith in community. And when trying our best to teach a child English, we might neglect to see the real stress of our demand, the child's having, in acculturating, to somewhat abandon and leave the people and culture she most loves and depends on. Our prejudices, even subtler forms, do their damage up high, down low, and in every layer of our classroom.

So what can we do? Though a complete plan of action is beyond this book, we can think of many things that might help. We can learn more about people we don't know well: take courses, attend workshops, and read up on multicultural education; see good movies and read good literature, including children's books, that reveal other cultures and perspectives; listen to colleagues of color talk about their work and students; listen to our own students and parents; and get to know people different from ourselves. We can also study ourselves, watching closely to see whom we call on most, whom we smile at, whom we encourage, whom we go out of our way to hear as well as whom we don't, whom we protect and whom we leave flapping in the wind.

Whatever efforts we make to better understand others and our view of them will pay handsomely. However, they don't guarantee successful and satisfying teaching. For even teachers of a child's own color and ethnicity must earn his respect and connection the hard way. To think that being Samoan, or knowing a lot about Samoans, gives us automatic insight into every Samoan is as far-fetched as the idea that I, a white male, comprehend and relate to every white person.

And yet as much as each one of us, even those of us from the same race and village, is unique and different, we are all much the same. The teachers who are most open to their multicolored students and their cultures will almost always be the same teachers who most realize their own biases and who most grasp their being so much more like than different from their students, however darker or lighter, similar or foreign. These teachers, too, will be the ones who see that all of their pupils need to be understood, confirmed, and liked. That is why *their* students learn best.

---

Earlier I said that in a perfect world we'd respect what others value. But perfection demands more. In an ideal world, school and classroom, we'd do more than just respect or accept one another. We'd actually treasure the diversity of what others embrace, and see that it enriches our own experience and existence.

# 9

# DO FENCE ME IN

IMAGINE A PROFESSIONAL BASKETBALL GAME without rules. Not one rule. Just try.

No time clock, no half-times, no quarters, better ball-handling guards playing keep-away from their opponents for hours on end, the defense, frustrated beyond belief, in turn, stealing the ball anyway they can, seeing no need to dribble, instead running circles like crazed full-backs, the ball clutched to their chests; bigger players controlling the play above the heads and outstretched arms of smaller ones; littler people, outraged and unfazed by the powerless officials, getting even by head-butting and karate-chopping those giants' shaky knees; the game speedily growing more unruly, less like basketball and more like drunken rugby, all the while fans, unbridled, throwing not just rubber chickens and octopi but rocks, bottles, and themselves onto the court to wage their own battles with home team bums and visiting heroes, mild-mannered fans and players escaping to the exits for their lives, causing disgruntled television viewers, soon bored by the predictable violence and lunacy, to change channels, the broadcast stations having no choice but to pull the plug, the sport shriveling up and fading into memory.

Okay, this is a bit of high drama, but not much. Without its reliable structure, limits, and rules, a game like basketball can get out of control just as quickly as that last sentence did. Ironically, it's the external framework—the stands where fans sit, the court where two teams of five players each play, the time constraints that bound the game, and the rules enforced by referees—that allows basketball to be played with abandon, coherence, and passion.

To function well a classroom requires a framework too. Children and teachers must above all be physically safe. No child or teacher can submerge herself in work when having to keep watch for danger. They must be emotionally safe, also. Who of us can take risks to learn when we are being harassed, humiliated, or put down? Though teachers can't rehabilitate every bad child or make every wary child trusting, they can take strong and careful measures to ensure that their classroom, *their realm,* is one that invites sincerity and openness, endorses basic human respect and consideration, especially for diversity, and has little tolerance for bad treatment of others.

There are, for sure, some children who possess self-discipline, good sense, and motivation to thrive in almost any setting. Such boys and girls can do good and independent work in pandemonium while other children scream, the television blares, and their peers run about. But that isn't most children. Few classrooms or schools have the luxury of such focused students. Most teachers deal with a more complex group of students. These children rely on designated seats and class schedules. They do best when told what the lesson is about, given clear directions, and maybe even shown the way. While rarer classmates may themselves be wanting and able to set the heights for their own work, the commoners do not. *Do we have to know this? How many paragraphs, how many sentences do our stories have to be?* Urging them to do whatever they are moved to do may well suit workshops on Haiku or tasks intended to joggle their perspective and creativity. Most of the time, though, making clear what we expect and when we expect it serves the children best.

But exactly how much structure and discipline are needed? The answer is the evasively guru-ish but no less truthful *we'll know it when we see it.* If we find that our students don't listen to us or frequently mistreat us and each other, or that we make excuses for their behavior, rescue them from consequences, yell a lot, feel like a nag, say mean things to them, bargain for every ounce of cooperation, let things slide until we explode, seldom if ever saying no, walking on eggshells so as not to displease them, or having too many moments (lasting days or weeks or longer) when we don't like our students, we need to toughen up. If our pupils are perfectly behaved only because we don't let them breathe, fear expressing an opinion or taking a risk lest we punish them, march in line to recess but show none of the joy that our colleagues' students do, and appear to be products of our running the classroom like it's a marine boot camp, our hand needs softening. When unsure whether it's enough or not, we go to the source, look to the only ones who know for sure—the children and ourselves.

---

In the best of worlds, discipline would be a minor chord in the teacher's repertoire. Our students would arrive at school with moral development well established. They'd have felt their baby hunger and cold soothed, convincing them, in the most vivid way, that their immediate world and the people in it are caring and dependable. They'd have known the warm glow of their parents' admiration and joy, further cementing that foundation of inner trust.

They'd come to our classes having been taught right from wrong and wanting to please adults, just as they'd know safety from danger, and see themselves as worth keeping well and protected. Having been disciplined with love, they wouldn't like the inner revulsion, regret, and sadness they feel when they defy us or break our rules. And so they'd behave well even when no adult is there to watch them, when we turn our backs or leave the room for a minute. They'd have known sincere and respectful parents who set a life of decent behavior for the children. And they'd have been given ample, virtually a childhood's worth of opportunities to exercise their judgment and struggle with their own ethical decisions under the watchful, guiding, and fair eyes of their parents.

But, as we know as well as anything, many children come to school in a different place. Some are severely abused and neglected, persuaded beyond doubt that the world is brutal and deserves their mistrust. Or they've been raised through harsh, impulsive, and sadistic means that have taught them to not make their mothers and fathers proud, and caused them to stop trying to be good girls and boys. Never having been loved enough to know they are lovable, they see all people as equally worthy of hate and mistreatment. Living on the street and through hard conditions has taught them to rely on their own powers and to manipulate others'. That's how they've survived. That's *their* resilience.

When we meet these children in our classes, they can frighten and overwhelm us. Sometimes their behaviors are so bad, so violent, or so defiant that we have no choice but to ask that they be removed and taken elsewhere, to a setting that can keep them and others safe, and that maybe (we cross our fingers with great skepticism) can do them some good. Apparently without remorse and without feeling for those they hurt, mostly from having tough lives themselves, these children can go off to futures as bleak and destructive as they expect, their more childish fears and dread having been chilled and numbed long ago.

However, we meet many more children who are on the precipice, who hang between the good and the bad life. In our own version of the battlefield's triage, we put our resources where they promise to help the most, in these children who, so close to despair and wreckage, can still be saved. With our left hands we offer these children our kindness, our tenderness, even our lunches, while our right hands corral them like wayward cattle, holding them as tightly as we can with boundaries, expectations, limits, consequences, and rewards. These children and their consciences are way behind and need to catch up. By doing what we can to curb their straying while nurturing whatever seeds of caring and remorse remain, we begin to restore the humanity that's been so tarnished or buried under layers of hurt and hardness.

Slowly, with hard work and some luck, we can bring some of these children back, our love and caring an antidote to their toxic lack of care for themselves. Though at first it's our prizes and privileges that motivate their improved behavior, eventually the incentive moves inward. As they take us in like cookies and milk, our wishes for them to behave and succeed become their own. We essentially become like parents who they feel love and respect them and for whom they might even dare to want to be good girls and boys.

Along the way we are also sure to meet other children who have not known such hardship or deprivation and yet who present problems to us. These are children, sometimes from otherwise good and loving homes, who've not been disciplined enough—spoiled children who get what they want when they want it, and who are seldom held to any kind of scrutiny or standard. These are the children whose parents perennially let them get away with everything. Whether they were uncontrolled because they were such adorable toddlers, or such good talkers and little lawyers, or because their parents were too busy, too unaware, too weak, we may never know.

We can help these children by finally giving them the limits and dose of reality long overdue. Glib excuses and slick talking won't fool us. Despite their gifts for gab and charm, we fear for them. We know that habitually excusing children for crimes and misdeeds can lead to their becoming adults who see themselves above the laws of nature and human consideration, if not the laws of the land. They, and their parents, may not like what we say today, but if we can break through their denial or veneer of superiority, they'll thank us in the future.

Should we wish to have an impact on our students' moral development, whatever and whoever they are, we must strive to be moral ourselves. What do our values say to them? Do we praise students more for *A*s on a project we know their parents worked on than the *B*s they earned on their own? Do we extol academic achievement above acts of generosity or good judgment? Do we put athletes on pedestals that exempt them from the mess and duties of their less-exalted peers? We must beware of our own deceit and hypocrisy, for no children grow well in such an atmosphere, and those moral lapses weaken, if not wholly obliterate, our power to nurture good conscience.

As many have said, give us a child's first five years and we can make him a good man. Teachers don't have that luxury. And yet we welcome and teach every boy and girl who sits before us. While problems of discipline will forever remain among our most hated, their remedy is often the road not only to a more ordered classroom, but to more ordered children and the better citizens they grow up to be.

---

Dew Wright is a good teacher. She's also a good disciplinarian. She doles out discipline fairly (never heaping it on one particular child, nor whimsically because she is moody or having a bad day), responsibly (taking the blame or credit for its effects), consistently (with sufficient regularity), judiciously (with thought and care), compassionately (with empathy for how it makes the child feel), for good reason (in the child's best interest), and with caring (driven by her wish that her students grow into confident, contented, and good human beings).

Her discipline is custom-made, using words the child can understand, appreciating what behaviors are reasonable for the child's age and nature, and employing time periods that make sense. She relies on time-outs sparingly, for they get old and feel rather arbitrary and somewhat alien to her, like sending a child to his room. What child, she wonders, actually sits for minutes pondering his misbehavior? She has met few in her many years as an educator. When she can think of them, she prefers natural consequences that relate directly to the misdeed.

She speaks what she wants to say once (or twice, at most), delivering her judgment early in the misbehavior when she is calm rather than waiting until her patience is exhausted and her discipline grows angry and vengeful. Having learned from mothering her own children, she steers away from empty threats and repeated warnings and counting to three. She knows these methods weaken her authority and make her students stronger, more persistent defiers who don't take her seriously or who just wait, continuing their antics, until the last minute when she finally means business. She doesn't negotiate clear infractions, for that breeds classroom terrorism, however mild. Nor does she discipline by humiliating. She can still remember what that feels like.

Because Mrs. Wright is in charge and administers discipline swiftly, she feels much less frustration with the children. And because she does it for the child's good, not because she is irritable or enraged or feeling jerked about, she typically has no need to show the child resentment or rejection. Believing that it's the firmly applied consequence that wields the power, feeling no compulsion to put on disgruntled airs, she routinely shows the just-punished child kindness and understanding for his plight. Likewise, she ever welcomes and sees the light in children's attempts to show their regret, make amends, and repair the damage.

But even as skilled and comfortable as Dew Wright is with discipline, she does what she can to prevent its being needed. She puts her greatest effort not into punishing misbehavior, but into promoting good behavior. She builds classrooms that keep children moving and growing, building structure and setting limits along the way as one might construct a road over the ponds and through the woods. While she isn't afraid to punish what goes awry, she'd much rather guide and inspire upward. She gives the children every chance to correct themselves, bite their tongues, change their devilish minds, employing her own wide range of raised eyebrows, ahems, stern looks, and nonchalant nudges. And even after they're caught, she often encourages children to hold their own courts, consult on the terms of their sentencing, and plot a course to do better next time.

Of course, even without her silly name, we all know there is no real Mrs. Dew Wright. And while she possesses qualities and skills worth aspiring to, is she really an ideal to aim for? What of her human reactions, her frustration when a child she cares for missteps or her anger when a child she's deeply invested in betrays her trust? Is it only undisciplined teachers who are less perfect than Mrs. Wright or is it human teachers whose passion for their work, and for their students, unavoidably raises their blood pressure, gets their gall, and leads them to get in a child's face or be anything but placid? Real teachers know the answer.

---

"We didn't become teachers to be cops," more than a few teachers rightly protest. But reality is what it is. For too many unfortunate reasons, educating children who lack well-developed consciences and respect for themselves and the world at large is increasingly becoming one of the most unavoidable, challenging, and precious of our tasks. So, to pursue that mission, we seek to learn better methods to contain and manage our students, sharpening our perception of when they're needed and our skills as to how to apply them. And, no less than the theologians and philosophers before us, we ever look inward to see how who *we are* morally enriches or impedes this critical work.

# *10*

# WARMING COLD
# SHOULDERS

L IGHT AS A FEATHER, bright as a moonbeam, heavy as a lode-
stone, dark as a nightmare. In its fullness it has prompted goodness and generosity, in its dearth it has moved men and women
to acts of evil and destruction. Cervantes knew what it was as did Balzac
and Hardy, Wagner and Lizst. It's at the core of Broadway, haunting
phantoms and orphans, and is mostly what Ella, Elton, and MTV's latest
sing about. It centers our fiction from literary to epic to romance to the
shoddiest of pulp and is what our athletes give thanks for when entering
their halls of fame.

At its best it can inspire the bravest and purest action, enabling mere
mortals to write the poetry of angels or endure the hardship of a dozen
lifetimes. At its worst it has led to self-destroying obsessions with cruel
if not abusive lovers who feel little in return. Conducting pseudo-psycho-
analysis from a distance in place and time, historians and biographers
have shown how its fulfillment and, more often, its deprivation have
been the force behind our great leaders and most demonic tyrants. Ex-
ploiting those who miss and seek it, evangelists and cults offer their own
spiritual brands of it. And more than a few companies, like Hallmark and
FTD, have built colossal cottage industries upon our need for it.

Of course, I talk of love, and not just the amorous or platonic kind.
I speak of the gifts that accompany it, gifts like admiration, understanding, and forgiveness, gifts that when lacking can hollow a soul, hardening
it to the love and attention that may come its way later in life. We all
know near saintly people who, having suffered the coldest of childhoods,
make a lifetime of giving to others all the love and goodness they themselves never knew. They are the exception, however, for it's usually good
love that begets more, leaving those who haven't gotten any more prone
to unhappiness and bigger problems.

It's this personal experience and relationship with love, and its absence or perversion, that children and teachers, rich and poor, slow and gifted, bring to school every day, and that has everything to do with their learning.

———————

*Pick me! Choose me! Me. ME. ME!*
Observe the eager children in any kindergarten or first grade battle to get their adored teacher's attention. "How much is one plus one?" "Why, can anyone tell me, do we need police?" "Would anyone like to begin reading our story aloud?" The content of her question almost doesn't matter as the children, like so many reporters covering a presidential press conference, cry out with their *I do*'s and raised hands for recognition. For all they know she could be asking for someone to give up dessert for the next 3 months or go to the board to solve Fermat's third theorem.

And what happens when she does call on them. "My dad has a white belt," one boy replies, having no idea what his teacher even asked, his amusing but seemingly irrelevant comment sharing what no one will ever understand as his thinking about a father who that morning left on a week-long business trip. With a competitive exuberance and blind confidence to match the most premature buzzers on *Jeopardy,* they call out, fearing that if they delay but a second, they'll be overlooked and miss out on some special opportunity.

These younger children have not yet been jaded. "Who wants to erase the board?" *I do.* "Who wants to neaten the book nook?" *I do.* "Who wants to build a nuclear particle accelerator out of the toilet paper tubes and shoe boxes we have in the back?" *I do,* would undoubtedly be the unanimous refrain. It's a rare child who doesn't want his teacher to borrow *his* pencil (when she can't find her own), use *his* baseball cap (to hold the names for the class lottery), or read from *his* book (when she left hers at home). *Look at, listen to, want to be with me, and just me* is their every wish and demand.

That children want their teachers to like them best is easy to see. Of course they do. Just because they're in a classroom doesn't mean that their deepest concerns stay at home or, like toys and Walkmen, must get left in their cubbies and lockers until they leave school. Whereas just a day ago they had Mom all to themselves, or at least, they and their siblings did, they now have to share their teacher with upwards of two dozen other children. *Love me the most of all,* each thinks. *Make me your most special one, the way my parents do or how I can only wish they might.* Each wants to be the teacher's pet in the biggest sense of that word.

*Like me better than any and think I'm the smartest, the prettiest, the fastest, the strongest, the funniest, the easiest.* In fact much of what children produce, in the early years and beyond, is meant to somehow please or impress their teacher.

These little economists, each wanting to monopolize the teacher and her precious goods, appreciate the competitive market in which they find themselves. They see her love and attention as a commodity, like gold, that's in scarce supply and overwhelming demand. Despite their parents' assurance, they don't see love as a bottomless well that ever fills. Love, to them, feels more like a pie that can feed only so many. They embrace the zero-sum law of love as the truest. If their teacher loves a classmate, there is that much less love left for them. Praise, smiles, understanding— all the same. Give some to him, there must be, goes the reasoning, less for me.

And so they fight it out however they must to get what they can. It's the law of the jungle. It's the law of the classroom.

---

Fourth-grader Patricia had a problem, and a curious one at that.

A bright girl, she had appealing qualities that should have attracted other children. She was creative, witty, athletic, and musical. And she played with the best of them, weaving castles, making board games and backyard mini-golf courses out of thin air and whatever junk was at hand. But her friendships were shaky and she often felt herself on the outside looking in.

She also had appealing qualities that should have attracted her teacher. And she could work and learn with the best of them, writing fanciful verse, reading aloud with flair, and ever offering herself up to do whatever extra help or project she sensed her teacher would like. But her relationship with him was shaky, too, and she often found herself outside what she took to be his inner circle of students.

Patricia was neither bad nor unlikable, and yet the teacher and classmates she wanted to like her most didn't seem to. "But I'm nice to my teacher," she protests. "And I'm nice to the other kids. They're the ones who don't treat me well. "It's all their fault," she claimed. "It's not me. It's them." What, I wondered, accounted for Patricia's predicament?

"I could ask her to clean and decorate the room," her teacher described, "and she'd spend her whole weekend doing so. And I have no question she'd do a wonderful job. Patricia," he went on, "likes to take on tasks that allow her to show off her artistic talents or that place her above the other children. When helping me she seems to see herself as junior faculty rather than as a fourth grader who is helping her teacher.

In those times she can be overbearing and the other children let her know it."

"They're mean," Patricia said, meaning the other children. "They act like they're your friend, but they're really not." Upon my asking, Patricia further explained what happened when she got the teacher's attention. "They're just jealous that I'm his favorite."

Patricia's problem was as common as it was formidable. Her utmost wishes clashed. She wanted to be the teacher's queen, ruling the classroom alongside him: do only what she chose to, enjoy privileges that were only hers, not having to do busy work and prove herself like the town folk. That is what she'd have liked. But she also wanted to belong and to be loved by her friends, the very peasants she yearned to look down on from her throne. She wanted her friends to be happy for her good fortune, celebrating her royalty as if their own. But this seldom if ever occurred and she was left quite alone with a wish that was more fantasy than fact.

What got Patricia into trouble, she came to learn, was her living out those fantasies, behaving in such a way as to pursue greatness by putting down classmates who, moments later, she wanted to be close to. Her wish to be all at once the most special and just one of the gals and guys, however, was not unreasonable. Why wouldn't she want both? Don't we all?

---

Eleven weeks into school and Jessica Levin could still no way, no how, seem to get through to Berry. Not that Berry was especially quiet or withdrawn elsewhere. She was well liked by peers and other teachers and anyone walking through the playground would have seen a happy, robust child. Berry was well-behaved and a strong learner. Ms. Levin could easily have looked the other way, letting Berry ride out the year. But Ms. Levin wouldn't do that.

A recent education school graduate, Ms. Levin was hired foremost for her enthusiasm and energy. "A dynamo" and "a firecracker" read her recommendation letters. At her interview she'd wowed the school staff with her warmth and clear passion for children and teaching. And almost 3 months into the school year she hadn't let anyone down. Coming in over the summer to prepare, she made her room as colorful and inviting as Indian summer. Her excitement was contagious and quickly won students and colleagues over, even children who knew her only from the lunchroom and the halls. If a popular vote were taken, Ms. Levin would have won in a landslide. But she knew she wouldn't have gotten Berry's vote.

As much an action taker and problem solver as a "people'r," Ms. Levin early on had tried to take charge of the situation with Berry, determined to win her over. She called on her more than the other children but that didn't thaw the girl, who answered politely and coolly. Invitations to share special activities, such as helping to make a Halloween display, engaged Berry with the task and other children but not with her teacher. Frustrated, Ms. Levin tried more direct tactics. "Is something bothering you, Berry?" she asked gently at first, over days her tone growing more pressing and annoyed as she got dismissive shrugs back.

Ms. Levin wasn't used to not being liked. This distressed her. Unaware that she was growing angry at Berry for ruining her perfect record, her hostility began to make itself known in disguised ways. She began to ask Berry more difficult questions, questions she'd have spared the other children from, and in a way—"Let's see what Berry has to say about . . . "—that trickled with a hint of sarcasm. She decided to stop trying to please Berry and to leave the girl alone if that's what she wished. Ms. Levin began to call on every child except Berry. She noticed little changes in herself that frightened her, that she couldn't even share with her husband out of shame. Why, she couldn't help wonder, was she now giving Berry's well-done worksheets a small check when her classmates were getting smiley faces and SuperReader stickers? And why now, when planning school projects, did she think about every child but Berry? The last straw came when on her way past the office she overheard the girl speaking her name to the principal.

"I think Berry might be better off in another class," Ms. Levin confessed to her principal the next morning, unable to take the tension any more. "And I know you must, too." Her principal looked bewildered. "I heard Berry talking to you yesterday," Ms. Levin explained. The principal looked no clearer. "About me, and how she doesn't like me." Her principal smiled. "The only thing Berry said to me yesterday was that school was going well and that you were getting a class rabbit. What's happening?" her principal asked, opening a long-needed discussion and a flood of tears.

Having shed her own sense of failure for having not reached just one child, and her frustration that a child could resist her charms, Ms. Levin was able to see herself and Berry more clearly. So lightened, she was able to let Berry be in a way she never could before, neither soliciting, nor pressuring, nor neglecting her out of resentment. She restored Berry's rightful standing in the class, be it with the praise or rewards she deserved or with attention fitting her behavior. And suddenly, like a rap on the door, she recalled that Berry hadn't always been like this. Berry, Ms. Levin swore that she now remembered, had seemed to like her on the first day of school. But she couldn't think of anything that happened either that day or later that might have displeased Berry.

But when asked, Berry could. With the clarity and vigor that was her, Berry told how upset she'd been when Ms. Levin had said that parents would have to leave their children at the school entrance. In preschool and kindergarten Berry was accustomed to her mother's walking her to the classroom just as she had that first day of first grade. That is what had hurt and scared her. Berry further told how she hadn't been that mad until *it seemed that Ms. Levin didn't like her* and was treating her bad. The truth aired, the impasse cleared, the year went on with Berry and Ms. Levin each other's biggest fan.

Of all the torments of teaching—and surely there are many—a student's rejection of us is one of the most painful. How horrid it feels when a child ignores or tosses off the help and caring we gently hold out to her. Understood and appreciated, such rejection can pass without harm. However, patiently and uncritically accepting it can be a supreme challenge. Sadly, our natural reactions—pushing the child, currying her favor, demanding her attention or tit-for-tat rejecting her back—can get in the way, force her hand and prolong the torture and her self-imposed quarantine. Keeping all roads open, especially those that run within ourselves, even when slow and tedious, can prove to be the fastest and shortest path between the child and ourselves, opening the intersection where we meet again.

---

Yes, it must be true that we won't click with all of our students. The baby watchers have taught us that children come into the world with given temperaments that may or may not jibe with their parents'. Some of us just fit together and resonate. Others can't connect however hard we push ourselves together. With some there'll be no chemistry. We'll feel nothing, indifference, barely noticing their being here or not. With others the chemistry will be worse. We'll feel dislike, disgust, disapproval, fear, and other negative sentiments. Oil and water.

Whatever the reason, a teacher's truly disliking a student is one of the saddest and most dismal circumstances. And I don't mean the dislike we all sometimes feel in the heat of the moment. I mean that which has an enduring, committed, and singular certainty. A teacher's not liking him can be a most powerful and malignant force on a child. It can bring out the worst in a child and cause him to prove that he's as bad as his teacher believes him to be. Who of us can function, no less think and learn, under the eyes of a parent or a boss who disdains our being? Believing as caring teachers that our first professional goal, like that of a physician, is to do no harm, when we find ourselves so disliking a child we are obliged to ask *Why?*

Because of the cruelty, meanness, and disrespect that child shows us or his classmates, others whom we love and care for. Or because he throws tantrums and things. She never does as we say. He mocks us. She makes fun of a retarded child in the class. He's bigoted and hateful. Sometimes we have undeniable evidence for our harsh judgment, our vision detecting true sociopaths and criminals who shouldn't be viewed any less sharply. Many more times the water is murkier.

Instead of reflexively running from Harry's eternally angry face and mood, we might wonder where it comes from and what it's about. Many angry children, we learn, are lonely, frightened, despairing children who feel helplessly small and insignificant. Children who can't accept any of the good help they need often feel ashamed of their frailties. The mere suggestion that they aren't perfect feels like a full frontal assault on self-esteems as thin and fragile as centuries-old parchment. More frequently than not, we'll find that the students who are critical of everyone else save their most vicious criticisms for themselves, their apparent disapproval of others being an overflowing of their own unbearable self-hatred. And in those tragic times when, despite the child's efforts to improve or other redeeming qualities, we can't seem to do anything to dislike the child less, we might consider helping move the child to a teacher and classroom where he stands a better chance.

———

Every instant, even during group and class-wide activities, teachers have a relationship with every one of their pupils, however much their own and students' temperaments mesh and collide. Though we can't always find out what makes peace and contact with a child, we owe it to them, and to ourselves, to try, allowing ourselves our forgiveness when our best attempts aren't enough.

# *11*

# SUCCESS AND FAILURE

IT'S NEAR DINNER TIME and Diana Roslyn sits at her desk. She typically enjoyed the peace and quiet of her third-grade classroom late in the afternoon when the sun still shone in. But today she didn't. For today she was doing her students' quarterly grades.

*96, 85, 99, 91, 78, 99 . . .* She enters the numbers into her calculator, adds them, and divides by 11. *92.* An *A* for Patrick M. No surprise.

*88, 78, 83, 79, 91 . . . B* for Shelia K. No surprise here either.

*Kerry W.* Ms. Roslyn, knowing what's to come, hesitates. She knows the girl's parents well. They aren't going to be happy, and Kerry is going to pay. *71, 68, 77, 81 . . . C.* Before entering the grade, Ms. Roslyn re-does her math, hoping something better comes up; of course, it doesn't. *C* it is.

As a teaching assistant in college, she'd encountered undergraduates who begged and demanded that their *D*s be raised to *C*s and their *B*s to *A*s, because their parents would kill them, because they wanted to go to law school, or, the most outrageous, just because they'd never gotten anything less. When Ms. Roslyn got to elementary education she believed that whatever problems arose, grade-grubbing would not be one of them.

And that was the case. She'd yet to have a child ask for a higher grade. But she'd had a number of parents do so. Some pleasantly, some less so. Though she always tried to talk it out, to find out why the parents were so worried, she'd seldom changed a grade. She still kicked herself for the one time, in her first year, intimidated by an angry parent, she had given an undeserving *A.* Doing so, she recalled, had done nothing to gain that parent's respect, and in fact, as she looked back, seemed to fritter away what little there'd been.

*Ellie T. 95, 98, 95, 88, 0, 18, 0 . . .* Ms. Roslyn did the numbers but she knew the score would be low. *56. If Ellie is an F student then I'm a kangaroo.* She wanted to give her an *A,* for Ellie was truly a strong student, but realized to do so would open up a can of worms that she didn't need. And so with confidence she wrote *Incomplete,* knowing well the problem her parents were dealing with; knowing, too, that Ellie would soon be back on track and eager to make up her assignments.

*Tyler, T. 71, 74, 77, 78, 76* . . . The calculator said *73,* but Ms. Roslyn knew otherwise. In spite of his significant learning difficulties, she and Tyler had made wondrous progress together. He'd grown motivated to do well and had advanced in every way. The sameness of his grades, all *70*s, perfectly reflected the constancy of his hard effort, steady performance, and improved learning. *B* she wrote, wishing she could give Tyler the *A* she believed he had earned, but fearing that his parents might misunderstand and heap more pressure on the son they, everyone knew, already had unrealistic plans for.

Earlier in her career doing grades had been an absolute anguish. Over the years she'd grown more comfortable—for example, no longer fearing parents' reactions to report cards. But even with all this experience, she still worried about the effects her grades might have on the children. She knew that grades meant little to her; she knew just as well that she couldn't safely make that assumption about the children and their families. She'd seen report cards sadly discourage children whose hard-earned *C*s were the best they could do, children whose work ethic and decency towered above the rest. She'd seen unanticipated good grades buoy children who hadn't believed they could do better than a *D*. And she'd seen a few unfortunately exalted by their *A*s, children who saw themselves as superior to the classmates who had to work so much harder and toward whom they showed little caring or respect.

If it were up to her, report cards would have been in the rubbish years ago. Yet she was a realist. Teachers, even the dreamers, typically don't survive and thrive unless they can cope with the reality that is. And so she did what she had to do to get by with grades. She did her best to explain what they meant, and didn't mean, to both her pupils and their parents. She tried to be fair and flexible. And most of all, she tried her best to do what she could do, reasonably if sometimes with compromise, so that her grades, which she seldom saw as doing good at this early time in a child's educational life, would at least do no damage.

And so Ms. Roslyn did her numbers, mostly for the record and as a ritual. But, of course, she didn't really need the numbers to know what grades to give her students. Her years of experience and days with these particular children had taught her just who they were and what they were capable of doing and learning.

Glad to be done, she closed her grade-book and walked it down to the front office, soon forgetting the scores and thinking about tomorrow's lesson on electricity.

Success and failure. Seems pretty clear-cut, doesn't it? But as every teacher can attest, that's anything but an absolute truth.

Sure, that boy earned an *A* on his professionally done geography project but, his teacher realizes, his parents did the bulk of the work. That teacher can't help but see so much more success in the somewhat messy, tilted, and less than perfectly accurate poster board that another boy put together by himself. Sure, too, isn't it impressive when a child goes through a year of school without misspelling a single word? But isn't it also impressive when a classmate probably doomed to misspell for her entire life, coming to terms with her significant language disability, adaptively learns to use a spelling checker?

Though they know that success is usually found at a *A* or *B* address, teachers have enough times seen success residing nearby *C*s and even *D*s. Who can they say succeeded more: the girl who, out of poor effort, slipped from an *A* to a *B*, or the girl who, doubling her study, went from an *F* to a *D plus*? Any child, it seems to many teachers, who betters herself in some way, arguably any way, is succeeding. Success, for many, is simply their struggling or trying, showing up for that dreaded oral presentation, admitting that they need extra help, and (the most common) no more than doing the best they can do.

Tim handed his junior high social studies teacher a coffee-stained and tattered yellow sheet of composition paper.

Mr. Tran looked quizzically at the paper.

"My essay on political parties. I know, it was due Monday."

"Tim, you understand I can't give you better than a *C* even if it's a work of art."

"I know," Tim replied. "I wanted to do it."

"I'll look forward to reading it."

As it happened, Tim's paper was nothing like a work of art. It was disorganized, the handwriting was barely legible, and the text was confused. But then, it was three paragraphs long, showed some actual research, and included a humorous jab that revealed some insight into the political process. Moreover, the many erasures and crossed-out words showed that Tim had tried to improve it. In short, it was light years better than anything he'd had ever handed in.

Tim got a *C minus*. But neither he nor his teacher cared much about that. Like the apartment hunters who can see a beautiful home behind the grotesque turquoise wallpaper, Mr. Tran was able to see the success in this belated, soiled, and haphazardly done piece of work. He could see that, however much punctuality, neatness, good topic sentences, and word processing were needed, meaningful change comes slowly and in baby steps. Time might prove him wrong, of course, for the depth and sincerity of Tim's gesture was yet to be proven. Losing a kid from education was always sad for Mr. Tran, but not doing everything he could to try and bring one back cost him sleep.

> Tim read the encouraging note that followed his grade and that praised all of the good and new things his teacher had seen in the essay. "I think we're headed to some place good," he read last.

Tim's teacher was able to grasp an iota of promise and hold onto it when his student was likely not going to be able to. Had he refused the paper, or simply flunked it, Tim might very well have given up. Children like Tim are unable to try and try again. When they try and it's not noticed, they are self-destructively prone to not trying again for a long time.

Honoring and nurturing such small steps toward success, however, can be hard for us, especially when these steps are tiny compared with the hill yet to climb. It isn't easy to get excited about a 10-minute assignment that comes in a week late (though that might be a positive sign coming from a child who never does her homework). We might not readily light up when a child who endlessly interrupts our class, with some self-restraint does so just a little bit less than usual or, likewise, when a self-centered child allows someone else to go first just once.

Some teachers, and some noneducators I'm certain, are finding this discussion tiresome and unreasonable, suggesting, so to speak, that these children rob five banks a week and then have the audacity to want us to throw a party the second they hold up only four. Come on, they think, get real. They're sick, they might say, of psychologists and pie-in-the-sky do-gooders telling them yet one more way to coddle what they might judge to be undisciplined, unmotivated, and irresponsible kids. Why should a couple of wayward children consume so much of a teacher's attention and be given breaks and rewards that the children who do their work perhaps don't get? This opposition and argument is not foolish and must be considered.

Adults typically don't change easily and only after they themselves begin to realize that they have a problem. Whether it's alcoholism, cruel behavior, not getting enough exercise, sloppiness, or whatever, it will not begin to improve until that one person, the so-called bad-doer, really wants it to, not in a casual or fantastic *wouldn't it be great* kind of way, but in a *my life's got to change and I'll do what I have to do get there* spirit.

The facts of change and staying the same apply as well to children and students. Some children are not going to check over their routinely jumbled and indecipherable math worksheets until they decide they care about it (or until they get the help to overcome built-in obstacles). That a dozen other children need only the teacher's raised eyebrows or a red zero on their paper to mend their ways is not the point. We're talking, right now, about the other child, the one who doesn't work that way.

And so ultimately teachers are left in a quandary. To at least try to reform that such-and-such child, they, with forethought and free will, might decide to work with his lying, cheating, bullying, disrespect, and shoddy work, accepting and acknowledging a bit less of the noxious behavior today because they believe they can live with an almost imperceptibly slow rate of success, a rate, they also know, that is about as fast as the child can muster. Not every teacher can do this, and probably not every one should.

---

Learning for learning's sake. The goal of all education. Teaching children how to learn so they can be self-learners for a lifetime. How does this actually happen, and how do we help it along?

For some fortunate children, meaning those born to good-enough parents and those born with good-enough biology, learning begins happening early. Often these children have parents who from day one prove themselves and the infant's immediate world to be reliable, trustworthy, and loving. Curiously enough, it is this early experience of being responded to and cared for, of being shown that what she does makes a difference, that helps to solidify the ground from which the child grows. These parents admire their child's first steps (and not just the walking kind), revel in her curiosity, and work to create a home she can safely explore. Her messy experiments with applesauce evoke in them the same delight she feels; it doesn't, as happens in some other homes, bring out their disapproval and sternly wiping washcloths.

In these early days children find two major forces propelling their behavior: the wish to please their parents and the wish to gratify something in themselves. More recent studies have documented what parents have long observed, that even babies will repeatedly shake their arms, make gurgling sounds, and grin for no other reason than the reward they know is coming, the crinkling eyes and glow of their mother's smiling face. Children who do not know this joy can find themselves at risk of becoming passive, needy, and depression-prone children who feel helpless and hopeless of pleasing anyone, or fear losing touch with their own selves, devoting their lives to trying to do whatever it takes to make someone, anyone, notice and react to them.

When children grow up in homes that recognize who they are, what they think and feel and do, without ridicule and undue criticism, they can grow to feel more engaged in their own lives, to be more active and less needing of others to give their life meaning for them. Their attempts to build Mom a lamp, despite the horrifying fear of their playing with electricity, brings more cheer than rebuke. Their love of reading is nurtured and not put down. Their interest in computers, even when it occasionally crashes the home system, is welcomed and seen as a talent and skill well suited for our age of technology. Their parents are willing to help, but have no need to take over. Here's the answer, we show today; here's how to figure the answer, we'll demonstrate tomorrow; and, here's a book that can help you figure out your problem, we'll offer the child next week.

Not that these parents don't recognize the value of a reward now and then. They try to use them judiciously, less often than more. For, they appreciate, children do love to work hard for not only smiles and pats on the back, but ice creams, special outings, and money. If all there is is cold cash, however, meaning something given mechanically, without pleasure, and lacking genuine pride in the child's effort and accomplishment, rewards will steadily lose their appeal and power. And, if they are overused, if children are accustomed to being bribed for the slightest bit of cooperation (for example, put your boots on nicely and we'll stop for a treat on the way home from school), they will soon enough wield the leverage of the mightiest labor union, working only when the conditions and pay are enough and desired at that very moment. *Keep your five dollars. I don't feel like taking out the trash and I don't need your money.*

By experiencing a variety of incentives, and by having their own early wishes to please their parents recognized and fostered, those profoundly soothing sentiments become part and parcel of the child. She now one day realizes that she wants to clean the cellar, work on her essay, or do well in algebra because it pleases *her,* brings *her* pride, makes *her* feel good inside, and helps *her* to avoid the awful feeling of letting *herself* down. (Of course, there are exceptions: children who, despite the least encouraging, most stifling, or least enriched of homes, are hungry for books and learning; or who, despite the best of parenting, care little for education and must be railroaded through every inch of their schooling. But while exceptions mean everything in the world to that individual and his family, they can't be used as guides to the understanding of what goes on generally.)

Based on their inherent nature and those years at home, children tend to enter their classrooms already somewhat fixed in how energetic or inert, curious or uninterested, motivated or not, they are. Teachers do their best to work with what they are given. By the end of the very first few days of the school year, an experienced teacher can probably point out the active learners. The task with these children is not so much to create a learning attitude and aptitude as to keep it going, to not squelch them and their love of learning. Those other children, the ones who see no reason to learn anything, are another matter.

But strong, creative, and determined teachers thrive on tougher matters. While they protest obsolete textbooks, unsafe corridors, and unceasing discipline problems, they are more than willing to take on the reluctant learner. Using every ounce of their natural enthusiasm, understanding of development, interesting lessons, love of learning, and uncanny ability to see even the dullest spark in a student's eye, these teachers, come hell or high water, will turn a goodly number of such children around. Being like good parents, these teachers will lend themselves to the cause, making clear to the child their pleasure and pride at what the child is accomplishing—or perhaps is just attempting. They will offer external rewards wisely and just enough to waken the child from apathy, weaning him off the rewards slowly but surely, substituting words for treats (*I'm so proud of you!*), substituting the child's words for their own (*You must be so proud. You did it all by yourself!*).

The sooner the rest of us recognize that learners, like Rome, are not built quickly, the better and sooner those teachers who daily live by that credo can pursue their important work with the children they love and worry over.

---

Most of us can't help but laugh when we hear that some New Yorkers get their just-born babies onto waiting lists of the more elite elementary schools in the city. That's so New York, isn't it? Well, from what I hear, it's becoming so Boston, so Chicago, and so a lot of other places too. But, I suspect, even the parents who fill out these near-prenatal applications would agree with our own shaking heads.

While standards can be a good thing, and we know the dangers of expecting nothing from our children, they have surprises and side-effects of their own. What does having *Go Harvard*, even if implicitly, embroidered on his crib sheet and diapers, overalls and sleepies, sweatshirts and wallpaper, do to a child? And what does it feel like to have parents want more than she can deliver?

Almost every teacher can recall families who, even when their child was in elementary or junior high school, made their aspirations clear. That their child was of average ability didn't seem to slow some of them from unrelentingly pushing him for more and better. Nor did their child's being of much less than average ability deny others' belief that she can become whatever she wishes (which equals all that they want her to be). What a burden to go through their lifetimes of education, not only feeling themselves to be less than what their parents want of them, but to ever work, work, work, never getting recognized for their valor, forever one or more steps behind the fast academic company they're forced to keep, and ever overwhelmed by the work they barely sustain by running on cylinders they don't have to burn. And even when these standards are in line with the child's intellect, they can steal away the child's inherent experience, teaching the child that learning is of value not in itself, but for the status, opportunity, and fortune it can attain.

Worse still are children who come to school with too little expected of them. Some come from families that—stressed, barely surviving poverty, having been little educated themselves—simply cannot see bright futures anywhere in their hard life or who have no direct experience to believe in an educational system that traditionally has been so white, so removed. Others come from families that, having known every advantage, have little energy and interest in a child who seems destined for what they see to be mediocrity.

When teachers inherit these children, they may find themselves challenged beyond belief. How troubling and painful to be the one, the life-saving one, who helps parents see that their child not only isn't college material, but that he has profound learning deficits. How frustrating and near impossible it can be for a lone and modest teacher to convince Mr. and Mrs. Corporate America that their overachieving pressures are doing in their daughter. How angering it can be to confront a father who shows no interest in his child's brave and successful battle with math and reading.

Teachers can do their best, too, to watch that their own prejudices don't get in the way, leading them to write potential winners off as losers, or, because of her name, or color, or address, to believe less in her, not envision her as vividly in cap and gown, and not see her as readily as tomorrow's leader, CEO, and teacher. Knowing also that such children—of poverty, of color, of immigrant families—can carry an extra heavy weight of their own, feeling themselves the family savior, the one who must succeed both symbolically, for the generations, and literally, to earn money and resources for those at home, teachers can help to hold and feed these boy-men and girl-women as they do what they feel they must, however arduous their journeys. And, of undeniable import, teachers must do what they can to help prevent children's being left in the margins because they are not classic college material or because they want a career not behind a desk, but one building homes, styling hair, driving a bus, repairing appliances, or doing something else that serves their interests, their skills, and our society.[1]

Though Dickens wrote about a London far from here in place and time, his caution that what we aspire for can be double-edged is still worth listening to. Wish or demand too much, and we can dampen or kill a child's spirit. Expect too little, and we can ensure a child's growing into the poorly motivated and low achiever we once mistakenly saw him to be. Parent or teacher, the lessons of our great and not so great expectations applies to us both.

———————

"Pass your papers up, please," Tamara Sanders asked, collecting them from her third grade class. "Write a story about something wonderful," she'd directed her students. "It can be about anything you wish. But it must be about something wonderful. Something special or magical." Watching their earnest work had pleased her for she'd hoped the assignment would fit well into their school-wide curriculum unit on fairy tales and myths of the world.

But Lucas, she'd noticed, hadn't written anything. A bright enough child, Lucas, she was well aware, had little confidence in his abilities. He did well on straightforward tasks, like adding numbers and fill-in-the-blank questions. He simply floundered when asked to create something out of nothing.

"Now, let's try and make up a wonderful story as a whole class," Ms. Sanders spoke aloud, as she ruffled through the papers as if randomly browsing them. Finding the one she looked for, the blank one, she looked up. "Lucas knows something important about wonderful stories. He knows you can't just write anything to make a special story. How many children thought of ideas that just didn't seem special enough?"

Lucas tentatively watched as several children raised their hands.

"Lucas," she said, walking to the boy's side, "would you share one of the ideas that you didn't think was special enough?"

Lucas looked at his desk.

"Tell us something that wasn't special enough for the story."

"A parrot."

"A parrot? What about it?"

"A parrot that can talk," he said a bit louder.

"Parrots *can* talk," the class know-it-all said.

"To people. But not to dogs," added the girl behind Lucas.

"What if the parrot could talk to cats and dogs?"

"Hey, the parrot could talk to all animals."

"Only animals he wanted to," Lucas said, speaking with a little authority.

"Only animals he liked, right?" another child agreed.

On and on, the children made up their own wonderful story. And Lucas had jump-started it all, his classmates' enthusiasm and wonder borne out of his self-proclaimed not-so-special notion.

"Great story," one child congratulated Lucas. "Yeah, I want a parrot like that," added a second.

Ms. Sanders was as wonderful and magical as the stories she'd been reading to her class. But she wasn't special in the sense of being rare, for every day in almost every classroom teachers do this most amazing feat: finding the success, or potential for it, in failure.

Regularly these teachers help turn instances of failure into moments for teaching, opportunities to take a step and a risk toward a new way of seeing, doing, or understanding. Not even the children devoted to proving themselves failures fool such teachers. With a steadfastness strong enough for all their students, these teachers hold on to their firm belief that most children can succeed, and that all children, deep down, want to. These teachers know that there's life after failure, because they experience it hourly. And they appreciate, too, the different kinds of smarts and intelligences that their pupils possess, seeing the keenness, the cleverness, the creativity, in the most obscure, seemingly failing, and most uncooperative places.

---

For most teachers, success and failure aren't opposites to be pursued or avoided. They are more a natural part of life and learning, the warp and woof of the fabric that is the classroom and every child. Seeing the failure that can tarnish success, and, more frequently, the success that can come out of failure, teachers help their students to learn about not just geography and science, but life and themselves.

## NOTE

1. Colleges, I think, are full of students who—over their heads, caring little, sliding through—would be better off and happier learning professions, trades, and crafts elsewhere, that ofttimes wasted tuition going toward investments for future homes, starting businesses, etc., giving them a true head start on their adult life. For all of this country's race with Japan, I wonder if the emphasis on college education is overstated and unfairly imposed on too many children.

# *12*

# DEAR DIARY

EACHERS KNOW THE STATISTICS about teenage alcoholism, drug abuse, depression, promiscuity, AIDS, and suicide. They also know about the other children who less dramatically fall through the cracks, children who, they are not surprised to hear years later, have turned out to have troubled and unfulfilled lives. They know these children need to be heard, and they know, too, that they need to start being heard before they grow beards and breasts. Long before. To help in that pursuit, more teachers are asking their pupils to keep journals, write reaction papers, and reflect on their experiences. And even those who aren't advocates of such personal writing, those disfavoring the touchy-feely in their classrooms, will find that some students, even if uninvited to, will write what is on their minds and in their hearts.

For even the most motivated teachers, however, this is no cakewalk. Carrying every aspect of human experience, from the superficial to the deep, from the charming to the repulsive, from the heartfelt to the insincere, children's journals can challenge the steadiest of teachers.

---

"An *F* in English, you?"

Ethan nodded somberly.

"How?"

Ethan handed me a black-and-white speckled composition book. I opened it to find nothing, not a word.

"What's this?" I asked.

"My English journal." Ethan explained that he was supposed to write something, anything, every day of the week, even on Saturday and Sunday. "By the time I owed 40 days I gave up."

I was not wholly surprised, for Ethan hated to write—for two good reasons. His mind worked much more quickly than his poorly coordinated hand, and he had difficulty putting the words he thought onto paper.

"If I go to your teacher on your behalf will you back me up?" I
asked Ethan.

"Back you up?"

"Make an effort to do what she wants you to?"

Ethan agreed.

When I called Mrs. Hodge, Ethan's teacher, I encountered a well-
spoken and self-assured woman. "He did nothing and so he got nothing," she reported sternly, her tone clear that she sought no advice from
me. "If it were my decision, journals wouldn't even be part of our curriculum. But it's not up to me. But, you should know, I don't consider
them any different from math or science. I'm not looking for life stories.
I'm trying to teach writing. And I don't treat Ethan any differently than
any other child. In fact, four other children got *F*s on their journals and
no one else has complained."

This told me what Mrs. Hodge thought of journals and maybe what
she thought of Ethan, too. But instead of condemning or arguing, I
poked around. "Journals are a lot of work, aren't they?"

"When I went to school we were told what to write and we did it.
And we learned our grammar. We knew what prepositions and gerunds
were. We were stronger, too. We didn't need a teacher's shoulder to cry
on every time it rained. And look at what happens anyway. You give a
boy like Ethan the freedom to write about anything and what does he
write about? Plain nothing."

I'd asked for an earful and I'd gotten one. And candidly, I had to
agree with some of what she said. But what I heard more was her anger
and, more so, the frustration underneath.

"You don't want to be doing journals."

"Frankly, I don't," she replied earnestly.

The next day Mrs. Hodge called me back. She apologized unnecessarily for what she thought was her yelling at me and then described how
she, unlike some of her colleagues, was never very good at "doing feelings." Though knowing herself to be a skilled teacher, she said, she'd
long ago realized she wasn't going to be the warm, fuzzy one who children leaned on. "They have their mothers for that."

"Check it out." Ethan handed me his journal. I no longer recognized the book. Ethan had written his name across the cover in all man-
ner of graffiti, big, little, upside down, twisted. Even the white speckles
had been colored with red and yellow highlighter. Before opening the
journal, I could see Ethan had taken ownership. It had become his.

I flipped it open and could see writing on several pages. I looked up.

"Read the first page," Ethan said proudly. I squinted at the truly chicken scratch scrawl before me. "Yeah, I know," Ethan observed. "My writing's the worst."

But I could read it.

*I hate this journal. I hate writing. I can't write.*

"Boy, you really let Mrs. Hodge know what you were thinking."

"Yeah, she told me to. She said to tell her what I really thought about journals." I went to hand the journal back to Ethan when he stopped me. "Did you check out what Mrs. Hodge wrote back?"

*I hate doing things I hate to do, too, especially things I'm not good at. P.S. Would you prefer to type your entries on the computer?*

I again scanned the many entries and saw they were all written in that same nearly illegible script. Ethan, knowing what I saw, explained. "By the time I get to the computer I forget what I want to write. Beside, I can use the practice." Ethan also told me that Mrs. Hodge offered to change his *F* grade if he chose to make up his missing entries, something he was thankful for and eager to do.

"She's a pretty cool teacher," he added. "Do you think that'd be a good thing to write about for my last entry?"

I smiled.

"Yeah," Ethan replied, shoving the journal in his backpack. "Me, too."

———————

Is confidentiality crucial? Is confidentiality key? Is confidentiality essential? Yes. Yes. And, yes. Even when they don't express it directly, children wonder what teachers will do with their journals. Will we show them to our colleagues, having a good laugh at their expense in the teachers' lounge? Will we read them to our spouses at night in bed? Will we photocopy juicy or incriminating entries to send home to their parents? We all hope that we won't, that we'll take care to keep to ourselves what the children have shared with us.

"Who wonders what I'll do with your journals?" we might ask, showing we understand their concern. "I am the only one who'll read them," we might continue if, in fact, that is the case, for the last thing we want to do is begin the honor code of journal with a lie. "But *you* can show it to anyone you want, because, like your thoughts and feelings, the journal is *yours*."

But what children really want to know goes beyond the legal implications of confidentiality. Can we trust you? Will you take what we give you to be precious and deserving of good care and protection? Are you strong and reliable enough to hear what we say without falling apart, getting angry, or turning away? *Don't be fooled,* their beginning entries seem to heed, *by this pathetic sentence about chewing gum. I'm just testing you until I can trust you are worth telling more to.*

While journal writing fosters children's relationship with themselves, it is equally about their relationship with their teacher. Most children, as if on the telephone or doing e-mail and letters, care about the person who is at the other end of the journal. A kindlier, warmer, more understanding teacher in the flesh will probably get deeper and richer journals than the cold fish who puts up with more than teaches her students. We all tend to tell more to those we feel are interested. Why bother revealing anything to a teacher who knows it all or could care less?

*Dear Teacher,* the children's journal entries might just as well begin, with the unspoken hope that she, upon hearing the mailman, will run to her mailbox, unable to contain her excitement at finding something— *from them.*

------------

We've handed out journals, or have asked that children give their reactions to some book the class read or a field trip they went on or to compose a poem about their favorite season. And they are coming back with writing in them. Now what? We don't want to walk on eggshells and yet neither do we want to be bulls charging through the china shop.

We comment carefully, wary of making the child feel unduly criticized. There are writings and times aplenty to learn how to spell, write a sentence, and organize a paragraph. I can't imagine writing back to a friend or relative who returned my letters edited in red ink. Our correcting what children write in their journals risks making clear that syntax and punctuation mean more than what they have seen, thought, or felt. Running their personal revelations through our human version of a grammar checker can reduce the good-for-its-own-sake*ness* of journal writing into just another writing assignment.

Praise, it may surprise teachers who like to give credit where it's due, also has little place here. External rewards can obstruct children's discovering the inherent satisfaction and value in speaking one's mind and heart, a prime goal of creative writing. Quickly learning what is liked and not liked, many children will readily forsake their true selves for false ones that please their teachers. And then what happens when the praise doesn't come? Children can't help but feel disappointed and rejected, wonder what about today's feelings is less fetching and worthy than yesterday's.

Would reading the journals or reaction papers without comment avoid this pitfall and encourage our students to come to terms with themselves? Theoretically it might but understanding this lack of response is beyond most children. Our students need our confirming and guiding input. Our failing to react would leave them feeling ignored and abandoned, instead of respected and empowered, causing some to reject their own writing, and maybe their self-exploration, as an empty exercise.

Our surest way is to respond where they are, restating little more than what they've said themselves. "Yes, what a trying day!" "I hope your dog's leg is okay." "You're not the only one to think the book boring." "Just as you said, we did have oatmeal cookies for snack." Being authentically listened to and heard is the most compelling means to inspire better and more communicating.

But responding empathically is an ideal fraught with danger. None of us empathizes equally well with all children and all experiences. Like most people, teachers can hear some things better than others. We usually respond to feelings-rich comments (e.g., "I miss my grandmother") more than to those toting facts ("My pencils are yellow"). And on the average we are more eager to validate loving or sad revelations ("I love you, Mrs. Valentine") than hostile and distancing ones. How many of us can remark, "Yes, I understand why you'd prefer any teacher to me" or "Tell me all the reasons you *didn't* enjoy the class trip to hear the classical music"? Empathy is a good thing. But what if, like praise, it's here today, gone tomorrow?

As our students grow more comfortable with their writing, we may dare to venture one toe out, offering some consoling, educating, or help. We may wish to disclose, replying to a grief-ridden tale, that in our childhood, we too lost a pet we loved. Or we may gently ask our own question back—"Have you tried telling him?"—to a child writing of his hurt that his divorced father forgot his birthday. We even may find ourselves, on rare occasions, approaching a child directly, offering some kind words or to respond to something she said. Attending to our goal of promoting their openness to and skills at writing, we may encourage them to tell more, further develop an idea or think about something in a new and different way. And, for tasks when we feel the need to correct the mechanics—the spelling, the structure, the content—we'll do so lightly, lest we unintentionally demean or overlook the spirit and substance of the child's creation.

While more tactful and sensitive teachers, those who typically intervene wisely, may be more natural at giving feedback that supports and encourages the child's writing, any of us who wish to can learn and grow into the job.

———————

*I'm quitting (sob). I can't do anything right (sob). I forgot to get my grades in and my principal was mad at me (sob). And I was so numb at that meeting (I get so nervous, sob). Even the lunch ladies think I'm a big dope.*

*Ruthie read out loud to the class for the first time today!*

*I can't take one more $#@$% minute of this $#@$% school.*

*I need a lawyer, fast. I said something really stupid at a child's conference and I think I'm going to get sued. Right after I get fired.*

*Reed loved his sneakers. I feared his mother would be offended but she wasn't. And he loved them. I watched his little blue feet dashing around the playground at recess. It's not fair that I have so much and others have so little.*

*That %$#$% computer. I lost all of my curriculum work. Three hours work down the $#$% toilet.*

*I'm going to kill that kid. If he ruins one more thing in that classroom I'm going to ruin him.*

*Why can't I just get a job as a gardener who works out in the fresh air and sunshine? Nineteen of my 23 all sick, sneezing, coughing. Their spit and phlegm is everywhere. Why don't they just tie me to the floor and inject me with every virus known to man?*

*Yes. Yes! My class did the best on the . . .*

*Cripes! What a disaster. My class was the only class out of control at the school play.*

*Mr. White [a child's father] is a total jerk.*

*I'm a total jerk.*

*I ate lunch with the kids. They called them wonder bites. I don't even want to wonder what might be in them. Sitting next to Mr. Sar-*

*dine Man didn't help either. And that awful cheese powder in the green tube. I swear I'll never forget to pack a lunch again.*

What, we are left to wonder, might teachers write if they kept journals?

———

Kathleen's parents couldn't understand their daughter's changed mood. She'd grown sullen and pulled into herself. She'd also developed a facial tic in which she twisted her mouth to the side, somehow forcing her eyes closed. Their answer came, accidentally, when they discovered a sheet of yellow composition paper squashed in a pocket of their daughter's raincoat.

*The thing I'm thinking about today is Fred, my dead turtle. He died on the wall. My father thinks he got lost and dried to the wall. I think maybe I hate turtles.*

That Kathleen, more than a year later, still thought about Fred surprised Mr. and Mrs. Hernandez. Why, she hadn't shed a single tear or spoken a sad word about Fred back then.

"Look," Mrs. Hernandez pointed to the red handwriting at the bottom of the page.

*Where's our sunshine? Think good stories.*

[signed, a happy face]

That night Kathleen's parents showed her the paper they'd found. Saying nothing, she turned away and crunched her mouth and face tightly.

"What is it?" her mother asked.

A single tear fell down Kathleen's cheek. Then a second. Suddenly, she let her body fall into her mother's lap, where she cried all the grief she'd held in for 13 months, and where she poured out how she felt responsible for killing Fred. "I didn't feed him that morning." She spoke, too, of her bigger fear that she might kill another turtle or, worse, the puppy she longed for. She even worried that she or her parents, or her baby brother, the one she sometimes hated, might dry up and die. Kathleen also described how she wanted to tell someone, how she needed to tell someone. "But Ms. Fazer didn't like my story," Kathleen said. "She told me that big girls don't cry in school."

"And so you stopped crying," Kathleen's father said. Kathleen nodded, adding how she figured out that if she squeezed her face hard enough, the tears and thoughts about Fred went away.

*Dear Kathleen,*
   *It was very brave of you to share what happened to Fred and your story about his dying. I once lost a goldfish and believed it was my fault, too. I am especially glad you didn't give up on writing. If we can't write about what we really feel, what can we write about?*

I wish I could say that Kathleen gave Ms. Fazer another chance, and that Ms. Fazer, learning her lesson, replied like this. But that never happened. Being the good girl she was, Kathleen kept writing in her journal but only things she didn't really feel deeply about.

———————

Knowing and liking oneself is the bedrock of good self-esteem and a healthy adult life. By experiencing and internalizing our acceptance of what's written, creative writing and journals can help children learn to confirm themselves. When we value and take students' thoughts and feelings seriously, such exercises encourage children to think and feel more, and to take themselves seriously. And by our inherent embrace of who the children are, all forms of personal writing help children to respect and grow more connected to themselves—and others, we hope, for a lifetime.

# 13

# WHAT'S THE NUMBER FOR 911?

*Dear red balloon,*
    *Dumb stupid red balloon it's your own fault you got lost. It's your own stupid fault. Even your mother and father are happy you are gone because they hate you. They wish you were dead you stupid ugly balloon. Everyone would be happier if you died.*

*Your friend,*
*Simone*

HAVING ASKED HIS FOURTH GRADERS to write their re-action to the movie *The Red Balloon,* Mr. Freirich read through the papers again. "I love the red balloon." "I wish I had a balloon that loved me." "Can we see more movies like this?" "I think the boy and his balloon live happily ever after." He'd even tallied the count. Nineteen rave reviews, three playful *I want to pop the balloon* commentaries, and Simone, the lone dissenter.

The 9-year-old's response wholly blind-sided the first-year teacher. Fresh out of graduate school, Mr. Freirich had looked forward to show-ing his students the film he'd loved as a child. The cinematic fantasy of a balloon that devotedly follows a boy around Paris, he imagined, would delight them. And they all seemed to enjoy it, even Simone, though now, in retrospect, Mr. Freirich doubted his memory.

Recognizing that his concern was rising to urgent worry, Mr. Freir-ich walked (more like ran) down the hall to consult Mrs. Manning, a special education coordinator. Though he'd been at the school for only a few months, Mr. Freirich could see that she was an intelligent and seasoned veteran, and, unlike some others, a woman who seemed not to mind his many questions about the school, his students, and teaching in general.

Gesturing for Mr. Freirich to sit down, Mrs. Manning calmly read the story about the hated balloon then, peering over her half-glasses, listened to the young teacher's pressured account. "Come after school and we'll talk," she said.

"But what if something happens before . . . "

"She'll be okay." Mrs. Manning's voice sounded as if she believed what she said. "We'll talk soon."

Mr. Freirich walked back to his class, reassured. Mrs. Manning knows what's going on, he told himself, and she doesn't seem panicked. But by the time his students filed back in from recess, he felt as troubled as ever. For the rest of the day he went through the motions of teaching, saving his real attention for Simone. He studied her every move and didn't like what he saw. Sure, her "I need help" ostensibly asked for his assistance on a math problem, but there was something deeper in her appeal. Surely, too, she often looked around the room during seat work; yet today, she appeared more lost, more despairing. And yes, she could be irritable, but this afternoon she complained too loudly about George, a classmate. *If only the school day would hurry up and end.*

"What's going on, Derek?" Mrs. Manning asked. She'd patiently listened to his anxious description of Simone's worrisome behavior and his sense that she suffered from poor self-esteem. "What are you really worried about?" Mrs. Manning repeated, looking him in the eye, stolidly unmoving in her chair.

A more subdued Mr. Freirich squinted his eyes and looked away.

"That she'll kill herself? Is that it?"

Mr. Freirich nodded sadly.

"That is a horrible thought, isn't it. Almost unspeakable," she added.

Mr. Freirich nodded again.

"Tell me about Simone."

"When I got back from your office, . . . "

"No," Mrs. Manning interrupted, "I mean before today."

Mr. Frierich portrayed a complex child who was of average intelligence, well liked, and a good student.

"Depressed?"

"Not till today."

"And today?"

As Mr. Frierich spelled out the girl's request for help (*Mrs. Manning: Is she typically a more independent worker? Mr. Frierich: Not in math.*), her being distracted (*Mrs. M: Unusual? Mr. F.: Not at all.*), and her impatience with her classmate (*Mrs. M: George? He's been on a rampage lately, hasn't he?*), all of his observations, the ones that seemed so certain just minutes ago, fell to the wayside. "Could I have been seeing what wasn't there?" Mr. Frierich asked.

"You had good reason for your worry. Let's not dismiss it too easily," Mrs. Manning replied as she picked up Simone's letter.

Mrs. Manning led Mr. Frierich through the story about the stupid balloon, line by line, word by word. Together they noted much of interest: the *Dear Balloon,* suggesting an affection and compassion to contrast with the cruel content of the letter itself; the *Your friend,* suggesting an attachment, a relationship, and a belief, perhaps, that Simone felt worthy enough to be someone's friend; and, the several erasure marks and corrections, indicating the girl's caring about her work, still wanting to please her teacher. But that unmistakably hateful and murderous message remained, a message that, one could not miss, was pointed, not at a dumb old balloon but at the author herself, Simone.

Less frightened, Mr. Frierich thought outloud. "Maybe I'll call her parents just to ask how things have been going in general. I don't want to go scaring everyone for no good reason." Mrs. Manning agreed.

The next day Mrs. Manning walked out to the playground, where she met Mr. Frierich.

"Her hamster escaped yesterday morning," he said.

"And?" Mrs. Manning surveyed the crowd of playing children for their Simone.

"Her father ripped into her. Blamed her for leaving the cage open."

"She doesn't look much like a killer, does she?" Mrs. Manning replied, sighting the girl who joyfully swung with her friends.

"Her father felt so bad about the whole thing that he said he almost came to school to apologize to her. Even turned out the hamster came back. I guess I got all wound up over nothing."

Mrs. Manning turned to give her sternest look.

"I didn't?" Mr. Frierich asked.

Mrs. Manning's frown disappeared into her own good-housekeeping smile of approval, one that would one day become her young teacher's, too, for he, she knew, would soon be helping other teachers sort their own worries out, herself included.

---

Unhappily, as we all soon enough discover, not every situation ends as neatly and satisfyingly as Simone's and her caring teacher's.

*A huge, heavily black outlined forearm extends across the oversized manila drawing paper. On the far right side a tattooed yellow heart,*

*split in half by a zigzag crack, the sign of its being broken, covers ap-*
*parently once bulging, now sunken biceps. Directly beneath that un-*
*usual adornment lies a second tattoo: a green serpent whose scaly body*
*twists into angular letters spelling out the word SORRY. Several jag-*
*ged lines traverse the exposed wrist, flanking a broader one in the*
*middle from which large, bright red drops of blood drip into a puddle*
*lying under the hand at the bottom of the page. In the upper left-*
*hand corner is a relatively small pencil sketch of a boy rowing a boat*
*against overwhelming waves.*

When teachers get a drawing like this one, they understandably feel
a sense of urgency. Only a removed or uncaring person wouldn't. Perhaps more than any others, teachers are aware of the enormous stresses
and perils that strain today's children. We know that children really do
kill themselves. And we know when seeing something like this that all's
not well. But what then can we do?

Foremost, we strive to take no hasty action. Though a drawing like
this is a cry for help, we remind ourselves that it's only a drawing. Artistic
expression, like thoughts and feelings, is not the same as deeds. A suicidal
thought, story, or sculpture is no more a real suicide than is a momentary,
angered wish for someone's harm a crime to be reported and punished.

Though we may be tempted to confront the student on the spot,
we refrain. The very nature of art, inviting spontaneity and tapping the
inner, more primitive aspects of human nature, calls to the visible surface
the rougher and gloomier aspects of life—dark and cold loneliness, unbridled aggression, venomous hate, frightening sexual confusion, and all
of the other stuff that has fueled the most wondrous productions of both
great and not so great artists.

And so, we pause on the possibility that such a drawing doesn't indi-
cate a suicide about to happen, but reflects our student's feeling safe
enough to confess some of his turmoil, turmoil that is becoming a sad
but true landmark on the adolescent landscape. If we, and our class, are
serving that psychological function, the last thing we want to do is expose that cover and take away that refuge.

We take note, and observe. Does our young artist's demeanor match
his drawing? Does he seem, in real life, isolated or distraught? How do
the facts of his school life jibe with his masterpiece? Does he seem to
watch for our reaction with sadistic pleasure or does the act of drawing
it seem to brighten his mood? (Sharing such heavy feelings can lighten
one's load.) How does the drawing compare with previous works? Is it
out of character, a more upsetting though coherent evolution of his work
to date, or, perhaps, an understandable progression in his trust of us and

his capacity to draw what he feels? Children often reveal themselves layer by layer, testing for their parents' or teachers' reaction as each petal of the self unfurls.

Teachers also must be beware of becoming too much of a child's confidant. Being asked into a child's secret world is flattering and enticing. But we avoid being pulled in too quickly and wholly. One of us has to keep a foot on the steady floor. A lonely child who sees that his bizarre and revealing work fascinates his teacher may unconsciously be moved to yet weirder and more disturbing examples. And if that student wishes to tell us something about his suicidal or otherwise worried thoughts, we cannot promise not to tell others, such as his parents. To do so is dangerous, puts the child at risk, and leaves ourselves on a very high and thin legal tightrope should anything go wrong.

Ultimately, having settled ourselves, we *promptly* seek consultation. We talk it over with someone—another teacher, an administrator, or a counselor—whose judgment we trust, and who we know can be discreet and refrain from pursing premature and ill-considered steps. We use this shoulder and ear to allow ourselves to fully feel just how frightened we are. We let ourselves think about what it is that frightens us. We are liable to act in useless, if not downright harmful, ways because we're afraid of getting into trouble, or because we misunderstand our anxiety about the child.

When we feel we've carefully and sufficiently thought about the situation, we act prudently. We may need to talk with a parent, who can shed light on a child's current upset or who can make decisions about therapy and other professional help. We and other school staff may actively help parents problem-solve as to what options exist and what path to take next.

In most cases we may wish to talk with the child to let him know we'll be calling his parents. We talk slowly, making clear our reluctance to breach his trust and expose his artwork, giving him plenty of time to speak on his own behalf, perhaps even complaining of what feels to be our intruding and betraying them. While inside he may feel relieved and grateful, he may feel compelled to vow that he will never show us anything again. Our steady understanding is all we can respond with here, and all that is needed in such difficult times.

Of course, if we fear that the child is being sexually or physically abused, our approach will be more vigorous and speedy. Some states, like my own Massachusetts, have laws that require teachers to officially report instances when they have reason to suspect abuse or neglect. Similarly, if we think the child is doing something illegal, we may feel impelled to do more. However, even in these more unsettling circumstances, we usually will profit by the thought-provoking care we have already exercised, enabling us to take good, not just quick, action. Although we may ultimately discover that some parents can't be relied on as good caretakers or trustworthy reporters of the child's life outside of school, considering all perspectives can only help us to proceed on surer footing.

Teaching is a hard job. But teachers who are willing to listen, who prove themselves to be trusty and worthy confidants, surely will encounter much harder times, for their students will come to them with their gristle and despair. Patient thinking, self-reflecting, and consulting can only help these teachers handle the crises their admirable traits are bound to invite.

---

*Ugh. Already?* Seeing the clock strike noon, Ms. Collins sighed as she watched her kindergartners pile back in the room from lunch, that half-hour break, just seconds ago, it seemed, looking to be her only hope. The hubbub of their return, customarily such a joy to her, hurt her ears. Their innocence and goodness seemed to disappear as she found herself imagining the evil behind their noise. Their laughter sounded like sadistic cackling, the opening and shutting of desktops became obnoxious slamming, and the not-yet-done chatter from the playground, angry screaming. Where did those 30 minutes go, she wondered, and how will I make it to three o'clock?

For what felt to be far too many hours, she'd worked hard to run her classroom as she thought it should be. But somehow it was all off. Few of the children enjoyed the story she read aloud; no one, it appeared, remembering the pages she'd read yesterday. Their making papier-mâché turkeys soon deteriorated into a fresco fiasco with frustrated children holding very large and oddly shaped globs of goo and newspaper, calling for help, a few tugging at her dress with their pasty fingers. Cleaning the huge mess took more time than she'd expected, causing her to rush and ruin the late-morning math lesson. She felt a flu coming on, and had a headache to outbattle the biggest aspirin. A punch-drunk welterweight hanging on for dear life, Ms. Collins hung to the ropes till she was saved by the lunch bell.

But now, not quite 1:30, an unfathomable hour and a half to go, the children lay back in class, this overwrought teacher sat at her desk, mindless, helpless, hopeless, and all alone, everything she'd learned in education school and on the job virtually strewn across the classroom, facing 24 children too excited about the upcoming Thanksgiving holiday, plus some other kind of bouncy and poky, as if smelling her vulnerability and going for it. No one listened to her and no one behaved. She could feel mean things, like "You little brats!" aching to be screamed. "What am I going to do?" her pathetic expression cried out to the little ones, who couldn't help her.

Like Ms. Collins, all teachers and parents, even the experienced and famous ones, know moments, moments lasting hours or even days, when absolutely nothing seems to work. These moments may be restricted to particular times, such as around transitions or on Mondays. Other moments may be specific to behaviors, such as students' distractibility, coming to school unprepared, or defensiveness. And other moments may be unique, evoked by a rare event or coming together of stresses that disappear as quickly as they came. Although such situations can signal a need for our intervening, our doing something, there are times when we just can't do anything right or helpful. What can we do in such inevitable times of confusion and futility?

*We can call a time-out.* None of us can devise a battle plan while under siege, which is why generals plot their strategies sheltered far from the beleaguered front line. We might take advantage of those who can provide some space for us to relax, cool off, and think.

*We can cut our losses.* If hours of effort have gotten us nowhere, why not take a hint? Conserve our students' and our own resources for a better day when constructive learning can take place. Let's try laying down the burden of being, for example, a good math teacher and let nature take its course. Taking the easy way out is not always bad nor is it always easy, especially for the responsible and, perhaps, guilt-ridden of us. Rather than struggle to persuade the children to do their work, Ms. Collins could have sat quietly and read her own novel, allowing the children to read or draw whatever they wished alongside her. The advice of educational behaviorists—that allowing pupils to indulge in their wish to not work, for instance, will reward their bad behavior—has its place and wisdom. However, occasional leniency in no way has to lead to a permanently wayward classroom (or home).

*We might consider that, sometimes, doing nothing is the most and best we can do.* It's not easy to resist the urgent temptation to take action. But haven't we been doing plenty of just that, and hasn't it, for whatever reasons, not been effective? When unsure of our teaching (and parenting) selves, doing less can sometimes do more. Far better that our students (or our children) ignore one more request to pay attention than that we repeatedly reprimand them in ways that are destructive or might actually deter their learning to take responsibility for themselves.

*We can beware of our frustration leading the way.* When our students (or children) behave in ways we don't like, making us feel inadequate, we can't help but grow frustrated. As the frustration accumulates we become less mindful, more knee-jerkingly reactive and at risk of resorting to punitive, even abusive, discipline. One more day of childish behavior will shortly fade into history; our mean-spirited words or coercive actions may not.

*We can try to think long-term.* In the heat of the moment, we can easily confuse our overall goals with an instant's demand. "If I don't get that boy to finish his story today," we may believe, "he'll never learn to write." (If I don't get him to brush his teeth tonight, his teeth will rot.) We might force the child to comply today but ironically undermine his will to work at writing in the long term. In this way Ms. Collins felt an understandable pressure to make her class keep to the day's agenda. But one day does not a year of education make.

*We can look inward.* Sometimes we do the right things, but they don't work because of our attitude, or because of what we're feeling. On the following day, for example, Ms. Collins realized that she had felt grumpy and spent, her headache being a sign of that before she'd even entered the school. That day, she recognized, was doomed to be turbulent.

And last, when the storm passes, *we can study the chain of events.* Let's observe what happened. How did we react to the student or class? And, in turn, how did they respond to us? We try to assess what words or actions helped, and which hindered. Reflecting on the previous day, Ms. Collins realized that she was angry at something a parent had said the day before. Enlightened by this insight, her stress faded, as did her headache, and she returned to school the next day the same old Ms. Collins her students knew and liked.

There are times when all teachers, like all parents, need to take strong and decisive action. And many of us are prone to let things go too long before we do what needs to be done. But at other times, even sometimes when there is an enduring problem to remedied, we will find ourselves ineffective, perplexed, angry, and lost as to our teaching. In those unavoidable times, our most economic pursuit may be to let things go—just for now, for today, till next week. By permitting ourselves that break, we may find ourselves better grasping our students' dilemma and soon enough knowing precisely what to do and *what will work.*

---

Nothing worthwhile comes easy. So why should the educator's life be any different? Mirroring the bigger life itself, the teaching life must have its share of bumps in the roads, flat tires, breakdowns, and crashes. The best we can do and hope for is that, when these inevitable mishaps occur, we have the strength to recognize them and the resources to cope and go beyond them.

# *14*

# ONCE ALL CHILDREN

TELL ME IT'S A BAD DREAM.

"Gretchen," the math teacher says, going first, "can some-times try but she just doesn't get it like her classmates do. I go over and over and over the directions. No matter how many times I repeat them she just looks at me like I'm from another planet." The teachers chuckle. *But she's a bright child.*

"Gee, I thought math was her best subject," a second teacher chimes in. He glibly describes some trivial things that Gretchen is good at before delivering his serious concern about her language. He reads off several examples of her misspeak. Everyone laughs again and nods knowingly. *What's so funny? You're talking about my child.*

"I hear that stuff, too," adds the gym teacher. "But what worries me is how she gets along, actually, how she doesn't get along with the other kids. I don't think anyone likes her. And that breaks my heart." *But her friends seem to like her, at least, I always thought they did.*

"She's a curious girl," says the science teacher. "She's just loving this unit on marine biology." *I know. I know. I've been watching her spend joyful hours working on her ocean diorama.* "However, she likes to talk and sometimes, well, I just don't have time for all of her questions."

"Well," the principal takes charge. "Let's hear about Gretchen's testing."

"I've finished evaluating Gretchen," the neuropsychologist starts out. "She's a very sweet child," she says. *Finally, someone who sees Gretchen for who she really is.* But the words grow bigger. "Dyscalculia. Dyslexia. Visuomotor delay. Executive function disorder." *My head is spinning. What are you telling me? Your voice is soothing but your words frighten me.* "Let me try and say it in plain English," she says. "Do you have a computer? Good. It's like when they made your computer they crisscrossed some of the wires." *Her brain is broken, is that what you're saying? That her brain is no good and never will be?*

"I understand that Gretchen's learning issues are important but it's my responsibility to point out some disciplinarian concerns." It's the assistant principal's turn. "She's late to almost every class." *But you know how all over the place she can be.* I know she has a problem with organization but if I make exceptions for her I'll have to make them for a thousand other children. She owes me detentions and I intend to get them out of her." A busy man, he takes his papers and walks out, angrily mumbling to himself about his being sick of parents who make excuses for their children.

The meeting, scheduled for an hour, has gone on for almost two. The principal indicates they need to wrap it up, but not before the music and art teachers and the adjustment counselor add their well-intentioned observations, which essentially second all that's been said.

"Thank you for coming," the principal ends the meeting. "This was very useful," she adds to a chorus of teachers nodding and smiling their agreement. "And we want you to know that everyone around this table and in this school thinks the world of your daughter."

"Oh, by the way," the science teacher speaks up as her colleagues stand. "Would you mind keeping Gretchen home tomorrow? We're going to the aquarium and I'm thinking, with all the kids and just myself, well, it might be a little too much for her." *Too much for her?*

I admit it. My portrayal is somewhat as offensive, unfair, and as heavy-handed as the teachers I caricature. But bad conferences happen. And, being human, teacher are bound to occasionally say unkind, impatient, and stupid things. And if we look back at what each teacher said, we'll find that little of it was actually in itself so terrible. And yet, none of us can fail to understand why Gretchen's mother felt as she did.

Let's take a minute to imagine what it's like to sit at the end of a long table, listening to professionals talk about our children—their faults, foibles, and defects, in ways that break our hearts, confirm our greatest fears, and that sound to doom our sons and daughters to a life of hardship and failure. Even when the problem is a small one and the teacher is impeccably sensitive, diplomatic, insightful, and compassionate, it can be hard and painful for us as loving parents to be told that *anything* is not going well with our children.

And so, when holding conferences or even less formal meetings, we try our best to plan what we'll say, and say what we must in ways that are neither sensational nor telegraphic, with a tone and attitude that is understanding and sympathetic, and with language that is accessible. If delivering bad news to parents whom we dislike or feel are uncooperative, we might prepare ourselves, by sharing our frustration with a trusted colleague, so that we can give these mothers and fathers the empathy and respect they deserve and which they'll need to bear and process the school's message.

At the meeting itself we'll first ask parents for their impressions, about their fears as to what's going wrong or what they fear they'll be told. Bad news that they can hand themselves is near always more effective. We refrain from hammering parents on the head; dishing out umpteen examples of the same misbehavior for pig piles risks overwhelming them. If we have nothing to say but one more instance of the child's problem, we might simply say we have nothing else to add. Our approach should be straightforward and geared to problem solving, inviting the parents' suggestions and help, aimed to the future and, generally, not at all authoritarian. And, we should leave plenty of space for parents' reactions, questions, and upsets.

Maybe, in the way that being told of their own cancer or having their own heads shrunk sensitizes doctors and therapists to their patients, teachers need to take that lonely seat under the judgmental eyes of their peers, to talk about their own child. Or, maybe, they can just think about doing so.

---

"I can't believe it," she said for the third time. Dara held the beat-up and faded blue folder in her hands.

In truth, I couldn't either. We'd met to discuss her teenage daughter. Working for a satellite clinic of a community mental health center, I was using an office in the local junior high school guidance department. Looking for a place in the crowded and small room to lay down her winter coat, Dara had asked if she might move one of dozens of piles of beat-up and faded, blue folders. I had no objections and so she did.

"Oh, my God," she cried. "I don't believe it." She handed me the top folder. I readily saw the reason for her shock. BEAUPRE, it read.

"That is a coincidence, isn't it? Are you sure that you want to see Danielle's record?" I handed her back the folder. It was her child's, but I somehow felt she was trespassing under my watch and besides I feared that she might read something upsetting.

"Danielle's?" She laughed. "Look!"

I read the tab again. "BEAUPRE, Dara."

"It's my folder from junior high. Almost 15 years ago. They must be throwing out old records to make room. Do you think I should read it? I mean, what could be in it, right?"

I nodded my understanding.

Dara cracked the folder the breadth of a finger and peeked into its darkness. "I can't," she said, closing it. "I can't do it."

"Then you won't."

"But I want to," she replied, playfully shaking her hands and stamping her feet like a child. "But I want to see it. Wouldn't you?"

I smiled.

"It would be easier for you. You'd just calmly open it and read it. You wouldn't have to worry about what's inside. You'd just know that your teachers loved you and thought you were smart. But I know that's not what I'd find inside. For all I know I'll read something like, poor Dara Beaupre, a nice girl who could only wish she was smart. How pathetic. I've got enough to hate myself for without that." With disgust Dara threw the folder back on its pile.

I wanted to tell this young woman, a woman I knew firsthand to be intelligent, witty, creative, and most of all compassionate, all of this, to tell her that her teachers never said that, never wrote that, never thought that, but I didn't. She was reckoning with her own self-doubt.

"I never felt smart," Dara went on. "I loved writing as a girl and wanted to be an English teacher. I loved my eighth grade teacher and wanted to be just like her. She had us write stories about everything," she continued, coming to life. "I remember writing one story about being a piece of driftwood that sails around the world." Dara fell quiet.

"What is it?"

"My father didn't think girls had brains. He wanted me to cook, clean, and take care of the house. He figured I'd find a good husband and not have to work. That's a joke." She referred to her ex-husband, an alcoholic who'd failed her and her two daughters in every way.

"And your mother?"

"She died when I was 5. I barely recall her."

For several minutes Dara and I sat in silence.

"I think I know what Abigail's problem is."

I looked up, wanting to hear Dara's view of Abigail, a gifted 14-year-old who'd recently developed a whole slew of symptoms including headaches, stomachaches, anxiety, and loss of appetite. An accomplished student, athlete, and musician, she'd grown gloomy and unable to take joy or pride in all she did.

"I'm always telling her how smart and wonderful she is. When Abigail says she can't do something or feels stupid, I give her a pep talk. Sometimes I get mad and tell her I won't have her talking like that."

"Your eyes are tearing."

"It's too much for her." Dara's voice tripped on her emotion. "I had a father who told me one thing. That I couldn't do it. And all I ever tell Abigail is that she can. It's too much." Dara sobbed. "It's too much pressure for a little girl. She can't make up what I didn't do. Just because she's smart doesn't mean she can't feel stupid or scared. Everyone does."

"Even you and me," I added, unnecessarily.

Having figured out a whole lot, and mostly by herself, in the doing so having demonstrated the very intellect and insight she feared not having, Dara casually took the folder and opened it. She read the top sheet, then the second and third until making it through to the final page. Nothing she read seemed to faze her.

"Well?"

"Doesn't say much about me. Though I did better than I thought."

I smiled again.

"I even got an *A* from Mrs. McGonagle."

"The English teacher?"

Dara nodded and gently placed her old school record back. Through this stranger-than-fiction life occurrence, she'd learned not only that no school record can capture who she was, but that who she was herself one day as a student had much to do with who her daughter was today.

Wouldn't it be satisfying to tell how that meeting rekindled Dara's love of prose and confidence in her intellect, propelling her back to college to pursue a career in creative writing? But that would be too neat and it just wasn't true. What I can report is that over the next few months Abigail gave up violin (she felt piano was enough), quit gymnastics (felt field hockey and soccer were enough), and dropped two of her *A*s to *B*s. Her tension eased, her headaches and stomachaches disappeared, and she came to enjoy school and life more. Dara was quite pleased and able to take pride, too, that her own growing insight and changed attitude toward her daughter had everything to do with this good news.

Of course, like Dara, we've all had a childhood of our own and each of us has gone to school. Though we could wonder what's in our own school folders, it's not those static summaries of our year-end grades and standardized test scores that tell or determine much of who we are. It was the experience itself, the days and hours we spent in our own little red schoolhouses, learning, playing, growing, coping as best we could with bullies, pop quizzes, algebra, success, and failure. How can that experience, the who we were as schoolchildren, not profoundly influence who we are, not just as parents, but as teachers?

---

"So what did *you do wrong?*" That is what my parents asked me in the rare times when I ventured to complain about my teachers. I learned early not to waste my breath talking about not getting called on, getting picked on, being gypped on a grade, and, the mother of all injustices, being blamed and punished for something I didn't do. I knew the response I'd get.

When I dared to share a tale of my making the class laugh, "You're going to get it and that will teach you not to speak fresh." When I asked how my teacher gets off making me wash all the boards for innocently doodling on one, "Good, that will teach you to behave." And when I described being what I thought was mistreated, "Good, it will teach you to get along in the world" was all I got.

It wasn't that my parents were such supporters of the school. Like most parents in my working-class neighborhood, they had contact with the school yearly at the fall open house, maybe. I'm not even sure that my parents liked my teachers or saw them as particularly effective. What they did see my teachers as were simply that—*my teachers.* That position and status, evidently, was enough for my parents. I never heard discussions about finding me a better teacher, nor were they asking me if I liked the one I had. The teacher I had was the teacher I had. A done deal. Get used to it, that's life.

That's not to say that the good old days were so terribly good, for often they weren't. I think back on my early school years and classmates. I remember boys who, unable to sit down and concentrate, ran around the room, climbing out the first-floor windows, literally getting into weekly wrestling matches with the school staff. There were students whose goofy answers we laughed at, all of us knowing which kids we could count on to be lost, oddly silly, and defiant. How many of them, I can now wonder, suffered problems with their learning, emotions, and families? The number of them who died early deaths from drugs, alcohol, accidents, and criminal mishaps suggests too many.

During those elementary school years cookies were a nickel and a carton of milk was two cents. At some of the better schools cookies and milk can now cost a child a dollar or more. But that is the least of what's different. Nowadays some parents ask their child each day how school went and what happened, forever assessing whether they need more or less help, more or less challenge, this or that teacher. *The teacher did what?* For every parent who asks what their child did wrong, there are four who request conferences, three who call the principal, two who show up in the classroom shaking their fists, one who's on the phone to his attorney, and dozens who, while refraining from action, worry about it.

But for all of our attempts to micromanage our child's education, childhood depression, anxiety, and substance abuse have been on the rise. Giving our children nothing but praise and smiley faces, sparing them every uncomfortable, demanding, or simply less than stimulating moment has not made for good and hearty self-esteem. By sheltering our children from life experience, we've unknowingly eroded their egos, weakening their strength to cope with the setbacks, criticisms, frustrations, and rejections that life hands them daily. In a cruel irony, our attempts to protect our children from pain and hardship have actually backfired, undermining their resiliency and leaving them more susceptible to feelings of inadequacy and despair that spiral downward under the slightest stress.

The pendulum ever swings. Psychologists tell parents to get strict, let up, and get strict again. Pediatricians prescribe the mother's milk, the bottle, and back to the breast. Like the up-and-down hems of fashion, the prevailing and supposed wisdom of parenting comes and goes. But whatever the generation, teachers can be sure of one thing: They will do their best to understand and to communicate and work with students and their families.

---

We could blame the parenting magazines and books for showing us what children should be doing and at what ages. But whom would we be kidding? Even without such prodding, parents take great interest in how their child is growing. Is she talking and walking when she should? Is he stacking blocks and recognizing shapes? Does she like to play with other children? Devoting all of our heart, effort, thought, and pocketbook to our child, we want to see results. What person can work at a job upwards of 18 hours a day and not care about the fruits of that labor?

And now, just because our children have grown big enough to enter school doesn't mean we suddenly put our apprehensions to rest. Good parents will continue to look over their children's shoulders to see the new math they are mastering or how their reading is progressing. They will confer with teachers to ask what they, the educational experts, are seeing in their child. These parents will closely monitor a specific school problem—a reading delay, sloppy handwriting, a lack of friends—no less carefully than if they were following up a suspicious blood test or studying the effect of a new diet on their child's diabetes. And they will want the teacher to do the same in his handling of both the child and them and their concerns.

Though we've met parents who believe they never give thought to how their children are doing, that they worry about nothing, calmly letting nature takes its course, we aren't so sure. Are there really such well-adjusted parents who simply take life as it comes and have come to full terms with their own limits and failings, who can watch over their children with an absolutely uncritical, unjudging, and uncomparing eye? Over time, when stressed or when harsh reality won't let them look the other way, we suspect that these parents will learn otherwise.

Parents will never (nor should they) stop keeping an eye on their children's development. As long as there are loving parents, there will be brisk sales of parenting books and watch-me-grow rulers on kitchen doors. By ever looking for the *How are we doing as parents?* that lurks in their *How are our children growing?* though, and by respecting and heeding both questions, teachers can help ensure that this measuring does not impede the very growth over which everyone sweats and toils, and for which we all hope.

---

When parents leave their children at school, they entrust their most precious things, their children, to the teacher. While transferring those small hands from parent to teacher can be comforting in the moment, its power is more symbolic, standing for the many years of all-important education to come and what, we can only hope and work for, will be a strong and effective partnership, between home and school, between parent and teacher.

# 15

# PERFECT TEACHERS

TO THE ADMISSIONS COMMITTEE:

*I'm no Albert Einstein (though I did do well in math and science). And I'm not the best athlete or the best speaker or the most popular girl in my school (but then not too many are). Nor was I voted the most likely to succeed, make a fortune, be in* People *magazine, or come back to our 25th reunion famous (surprise! the best athlete, best speaker, and most popular kids were). But if they chose the student most likely to care, I think I'd have had a good chance.*

*Even as a little girl littler children looked to me. Something about me, I'm not sure what. And as a junior high student I was (cough, cough, humility) one of the most favorite babysitters in my town. I had a knack for keeping kids happy and occupied. The woman who ran my babysitting class said I was the most mature girl she'd ever trained.*

*But I did a lot more than just take care of neighbor's kids (though that is, I think, no small shakes). For 5 years I've helped out at the Special Olympics (my cousin has Downs Syndrome) and the last 2, at our local shelter for battered women. I run an art class for their children. (Oh, I'm a painter, too. Paintings, not houses.) And this senior year I'm leading a group of students who find volunteer opportunities and then fill them with kids from the lower grades in the high school and junior high. It is a rip-roaring success.*

*With my strong academic background and civil service, I think I'd be a good candidate for your program in education. I work hard and care about children. I am creative. (Oh, not just with paints. I was vice-president of the Problem Solvers Club, too.)*

*I've thought long and hard about my going to education school. I would like the opportunity to teach the children useful things like adding, reading, and using a computer (I know some programming.)*

103

> *But I also want to teach them how to respect each other and their*
> *world. Too many children are growing up unloved. I think I'd be*
> *good at turning hate into love. (I'm not a hippie. My parents wor-*
> *ried, I should point that out.) By teaching my students to care like*
> *I do I think I could really help to change the world.*
> *Thank you. I hope to see you in the fall.*

Like taking candy from a baby. Wouldn't making fun of this essay be that easy? ... *Teach them how to respect....Turning hate to love....Teaching my students to care like I do....Change the world.* Why not just send her essay on a Hallmark Valentine's card?

Idealism unsettles us, doesn't it? Only foolish youth, we think, can believe such large and noble fantasies. Is she, a modern-day saint, going to walk barefoot through the streets, moving gang members to drop their zip guns and blades in tears, asking for forgiveness? More like some Mary Poppins, will she sing sugar to melt the cold and ruthless hearts around her, transforming their bad thoughts to good? Or, a 22nd-century multimedia'd Pied Piper, will she play her inspiring tune in every village, the billions of children marching sweetly and kindly behind her?

Not that we doubt this high school senior's sincerity, for that is the last thing we'd do. Sure, she's trying to say what she thinks the committee wants to hear. But she also means it. Besides, her vision of what's wrong and needed is realistic. The national problem of disrespect? She could document it as well as any sociologist or journalist. The prevalence of hate? Ditto. The need for our children to substantially learn what they need to in order to survive and thrive in this age of technology? She grasps that, too.

No, this admirable young woman is neither trite nor a cliché. Contemplating a noble career in education, she's setting her standards as high as the moon. She should, for the hard realities of the world will pull them down. Full of her own caring, she fancies that it will magically ooze into her students, infecting them with their own caring. Isn't that how we all learn to care? She will, she predicts, teach her pupils how to respect others. What she hasn't spelled out, but has already experienced, is the way she'll have to work at it, demanding it and even punishing its absence. Not out of innocence but through maturity she can see the hurt and fear underlying much hate, and time will prove her right, that she will be able to bring some angry and lost children back to life. As for changing the world? How else does anyone change the world but inch by inch, student by student? Rather than set her up for defeat and certain disappointment, her lofty aspirations will anchor and guide her, especially in the colder, darker times she'll unavoidably encounter.

*She's a teacher,* the committee agrees, hoping she chooses their school, hoping to find more of her, hoping she's real.


## PLATO INTERVIEWS THE TEACHER OF THE YEAR

*Plato:*[1] How did it feel to be chosen the best teacher of the year?

*Mrs. Droggittis:* I'm overjoyed. The work itself is rewarding but it's especially nice to be noticed by the children.

*Plato:* You call the students *children.*

*Mrs. D:* Well, I just turned 50 and you and your classmates just look so young to me. Though many, like yourself, are a head taller. [laughs]

*Plato:* What do you attribute your winning the award to?

*Mrs. D:* Good luck. [laughs] No, really, I think what children [laughs], students like is that I listen to them and I take what they tell me seriously. They may not always like my decisions, but no one can say that I don't give their opinion a fair hearing.

*Plato:* Why did you become a teacher?

*Mrs. D:* A lot of reasons. I started off wanting to become a librarian but soon discovered that talking to the children who came by excited me more than the books themselves. And if you asked me this question 20 years ago, I'd have said one thing: to help the children. Not that it wasn't true. It was. I took much pride in helping an illiterate child learn to read or discovering another's giftedness and giving her the challenge she needed. My classes, if I can brag a little, were always prepared. It was a rare bird who left my class not much ahead of where he'd entered. And they were well behaved, too. Everyone used to joke that what I really taught was etiquette.

But what I later learned was that, as much as I liked doing good, that wasn't my main motivation in teaching. I guess I've realized that, even though I'm the one teaching, what really gets me going is watching the children. I've become a kind of student of the mind. Whether I'm teaching writing, or math, or science, I've taught all three, you know, the children's thinking, the way they look at things, never fails to fascinate me. My new project has been to read all the new books about language, and then I compare what I learn with what the students actually say and write. I feel as if I have my own human laboratory to experiment and observe. I feel very fortunate. Few people have such an interesting and varied job.

*Plato:* You've been teaching for almost 30 years now, and . . .

*Mrs. D:* Ahem. Only 26, Plato.

*Plato*: You've been teaching [laughs] only 26 years. Has teaching changed much over this time?

*Mrs. D*: Oh, my, I should say it has. The children come in knowing so much more. In science, for example, we now teach subjects that used to be taught in high school and that I learned in college. I'm sure it won't astonish you to hear that your classmates are not quite as mannered as my students were when I began. Would you believe that my first class used to stand and say "Good morning, Mrs. Droggittis" when I came in? [Plato raises his eyebrows in disbelief] Can you believe it? And then, things were simpler. I remember bringing in a winter coat for a little girl whose father, a bus driver, I think he was, had been laid off right before the holidays. I wouldn't dare do that today. I'd be sued. [pauses] And, of course, there's all that new technology now.

*Plato*: You've learned about computers?

*Mrs. D*: Yes. I've been lucky. My son is something of a computer expert and he's taught me quite a lot.

*Plato*: Speaking of your son, [laughs] do you have a life of your own, outside of teaching?

*Mrs. D*: You know, that's a very good question.

*Plato*: Students like to know that kind of stuff.

*Mrs. D*: Yes, I can see why they would. In fact, I do. I'm an avid bird watcher and outdoors woman. We, my family, that is, like to canoe and bicycle and hike, too. I'm an adventurous cook and, my husband says, a mad reader. And next week I'll be taking a class on the stock market. That's always intrigued me. Not that I have a whole lot of money to play with.

*Plato*: Money? Do you get paid a lot?

*Mrs. D*: I'm not complaining. We have everything we need. But educators have always been underpaid. People think we have easy jobs, that we come into school at 8:30, have a cup of coffee, teach a few courses, and go home at 2:00. If I got paid, never mind overtime, for every early morning or late afternoon conference, meeting, and workshop, not to mention school and curriculum work I do on the weekends and in the summer, I'd be a rich woman.

*Plato*: And you're not?

*Mrs. D*: Not in bucks. But I am a rich woman in the ways that matter.

*Plato*: Like being the kind of teacher students have voted as the best?

*Mrs. D* [smiles]: Yes. Just so.

*Plato*: Well, I want to congratulate you and thank you for talking with me.

*Mrs. D*: It's been my pleasure. [pauses] Oh, by the way, Plato, have you practiced your trumpet yet today?

*Plato*: I was just about to, Mom.
[Mrs. D smiles]

———————

I loved some of my teachers. But I'm not sure they ever knew it. Well, they probably could tell, but I never told them so. When I'd come back from a vacation or after the summer break, I'd want to run up and greet them, maybe grab a hug. But I didn't dare. It would have looked too *un*cool, too goody-goody, and would have put me at risk. What if I ran to my teacher and she didn't care or, worse, pushed me away? Though every time I played scrub and stickball on the school's asphalt playground, I kept an eye out for those men and women, I kept my fondness to myself.

I know that my experience wasn't unusual. My children have loved certain teachers, but showing it, after the fact, has been complicated for them. "We saw Mr. So-and-so at the mall" evokes great excitement. *Who was he with? Does he have children? Did he mention me?* they want to know. But should they themselves bump into those same dear teachers out about town, they shyly look to their shoes, answering their beloved teacher's questions in monotones and monosyllables. Do their teachers know what their students really feel? I wonder.

What is the measure of a teacher's success? A child's learning to read. Another's learning to write. A third's simply deciding he really does want to learn. Improved grades? Standardized test scores? A raise? A letter of commendation from the principal or the school committee? Polished apples from the children? Gift certificates to the book store from their parents?

There is no one touchstone that tells us we've done good. Many times our principals and supervisors neither notice nor tell us, wanting only to point out the one of a hundred things we haven't gotten to or to ask yet more of us. Parents don't honor us much either, speaking up more to blame than to credit us and our teaching, aiming straight for what we do while making clear that what they do, what they contribute to the problem, is off limits. Though we crave a supportive *Look at all you've done,* we've grown accustomed to the less friendly *What have you done for us (and our child) lately?* And so, instead of the recognition and reward we deserve and need, we settle for bits and pieces of encouragement here, pats on the back there. We hungrily take them however and from wherever they come.

Sometimes, we learn of our success right then and there, as when a child gives thanks, or a parent acknowledges the progress their child has made with us. More often, we hear of it months or even years later, heartfelt notes of gratitude thanking us—*for learning me to read, for teaching me to care about myself, for helping me to not take drugs, for knowing I wasn't stupid, for believing in me, for being the one person who thought I was worth something, for helping me get to the good place I, as an adult, have now gotten*—letters that tear our eyes, tug at our hearts, and testify that the teaching we do matters. Though our students, recent and past, wish they could bring themselves to sit down and write us, seldom do these letters get written or mailed. But we, we must recall, are ever in their minds, just as they are in ours. We are ever part of them—and they, of us.

---

Many professions vie for the title of most impossible, but none deserves it more than teaching. Consider what teachers do each day, welcoming pupils, all who differ in brain power, learning style, motivation, concentration, health, and self-esteem. To further confound an already too complicated situation, on any day, at any moment, these children vary in mood, how rested they are, whether they were sent to school well-fed or hungry, rested or exhausted, encouraged or belittled, with a hug or a kick and good riddance. And on some days one or more of these children will be suffering something catastrophic—a family illness, death, divorce, or abuse.

What teacher can see all that goes on in a classroom of students? None, of course. To do so is as statistically unlikely as a nuclear physicist's knowing everything about the subatomic particles that race around her experimental cyclotron. Things in the classroom change too much and too quickly. Few realize what the teacher's work day is really like. For every teacher who runs out of school at the bell there are a dozen who stay late, work at night, on weekends, and in the summer, and who are ever on the lookout for ways to enrich their students' education.

If that isn't enough challenge—and of course it is—teachers must also deal with parents' psyches, often facing worried, angry, critical, threatening, or otherwise stressed and distressed mothers and fathers. On the worst days, they confront parents who, they fear, may be mistreating their children or attending parent–child conferences under the threatening eyes of the family's hired guns, advocates and attorneys. On the best, they teach in the heavy shadow of parental expectations and vulnerabilities.

And then there are the other little, big things: Working for days to calm an unreasonably riled parent situation only to have the assistant principal blow it all open again with a flippant, shoot-from-the-hip remark to the father. Meticulously preparing for a difficult meeting, only to have a fellow teacher undermine our hard and sound work. Or what about the those times we are left unsupported, if not totally hung out to dry, by our administrators, or when we, good school citizens who try to do our best ethically, are asked to compromise our way of teaching or to cover up for another's careless mistake? And that's not to mention our being questioned and criticized by outside consultants, every Tom, Dick, and Harry (and Sue, Jane, and Mary) who think they know more about our work than we do. Inadequate supplies, cold and leaky classrooms, and the excavation work that's been going on outside our window for 5 months now don't help much either.

In most jobs, years of experience bring greater comfort, satisfaction, prestige, and financial reward. Recent reports show that teaching is one of the few careers that has been going backward in terms of salaries and benefits. Though seasoned teachers are wiser and savvier, they frequently are asked to do more and, like their younger colleagues, face a public and classrooms that don't just seem to, but actually do get tougher year after year. Somehow those decades of know-how don't make the work easier, leaving some good teachers worn, wondering whether they'll survive, whether they'll make it to retirement. And dignity? For all the hot air that noneducators blow over education, and all the love our society professes for children, at the bottom line teachers, the ones who educate our dear sons and daughters, get little respect.

So, here at ten to five, the sun set, alone in our classroom, still not quite prepared for the next day, reminding ourselves to call friends to see if someone can take our own children to school tomorrow for we've agreed to meet a parent—an arrogant CEO who's too busy for everyone, most of all his son—at 6:45, filling our straining briefcase with papers upon papers to correct, articles to read, progress reports to fill out, we head for the door, still worried about the recent plummet in Racheal's work, still saddened that last night the town voted down the school bill, trying to swallow that reddening sore throat, knowing there's no way we could ever stay home tomorrow, as we walk glancing at the newspaper's front page article on how educators are overpaid and failing to educate students. Is it any wonder we often walk out of school exhausted, head pounding, feeling defeated and hopeless, wondering how we ever got into this business and maybe, how we can get out?

Teachers who want to teach know we'll have to contend with reality. But what, in the meanwhile and as we brace for the storms that assault us daily, can we do to protect and care for ourselves?

*We can set clear priorities.* We can try to identify not only worthy goals, but reasonable goals, for each day and the year—a workshop on poetry, a field-laboratory program for learning local plants and wildlife, a get-to-know-your-feelings curriculum. Like a child in a candy shop, interested teachers are game to take on more than they can handle. Every great idea or lesson plan they hear of becomes one more option for their own class. But one more option equals one more responsibility and a lot more work. True enough, we can't avoid some duties. However, our realizing what we can or can't do will help us to manage our own time and schedules. Any one person, even one fine teacher, can only do so much.

*We can listen to our conscience.* We do our job well. That is what we're paid for. Though we need and want to work cooperatively as part of a school community, we also must stay true to our values. If asked to do things that make us feel uncomfortable, things that are dishonest or unethical, or are just plain unfair, it's not only our right but our obligation to say no. After all, even as we balance the inescapable pressures of our job, it is we ourselves who ultimately live with our decisions and actions.

*We can heed our tensions more closely.* We can find safe places—with other teachers, friends, or family—where we can let down our guard, use words like *stupid,* complain without feeling like a whiner, and cry that *we can't take it anymore* to a sympathetic ear, one that knows we don't really mean it. Like wet sponges too swollen to soak up one more drop of water, we get saturated, used up, so we can't listen to one more question, call on one more raised hand. Getting away, taking a nap, reading a novel, riding a bike, taking a walk, practicing yoga, meditating, maybe even watching *Hollywood Squares,* can be the respite that renews us, as might a good night's sleep or a warm bowl of soup. Even more than teacher workshops, journals, and books, taking good care of ourselves can arguably do the most to keep us moving and teaching. And last, we can try to better understand what stresses us, for example, our tendency to feel put down or to volunteer for work we always come to resent, taking measures, when needed, to get ourselves help or to make changes in how we go about our life at school.

*We can realize that no teacher can understand and please everyone, or even any one person, all of the time.* However trite it might sound, teachers tend to be the kind of people who need people. Many of us aim to please others as vigorously as we do anything to avoid others' disapproval. In a fair world the meek would inherit, or at least our good and compliant nature wouldn't be taken advantage of. Unfortunately, those of us who are easy are often asked and expected to do more for less by others—and by ourselves. We need to learn to stand up for ourselves, and to have compassion for the times when our doing what we have to do displeases people. They'll get used to it, and so will we, if we try. By coming to terms with all we can't do, we'll come to more clearly see what we can do, helping to turn an impossible situation, and profession, into a more comfortable and satisfying classroom of possibility.

*We can try to hold onto those moments of triumph and joy that we create and come upon in our classrooms.* It might be the great excitement of our finally reaching that estranged boy or piquing that eternally bored girl's curiosity. It might be the satisfaction of seeing our class's respectable conduct at the school graduation ceremony, or the warmth we feel as our reading circle listens, eyes wide, mouths silent, captivated by our words. It might come in as small and simple a package as the children's all understanding today's science lesson. Experienced teachers know those moments of connection, of progress, of discovery, are what truly sustain and buoy them, moments they keep learning to better see, appreciate, and embrace.

Finally, *we can try to accept our being humanly destined to forever be less than perfect,* especially when it comes to the students we love and teach. We are all limited by our human nature, and by our sad but true inability to love and protect, connect with and teach students as well as we might wish. Despite how smart, informed, earnest, or emotionally healthy we are, like good parents we have the capacity to imagine lives for our students that are so much safer, happier, and more wonderful than those we can give them. We can fantasize wonderful worlds. But it's our obligation to help our students learn to endure the daily slings and arrows, and the more monumental trials, pain, and losses, they, like all of us, will know throughout their days in school and beyond, all the while teaching them facts and theory, reading and writing, the value of education and the value of their selves.

We do all this, and more, whenever we do that thing called teaching.

---

Like perfect children and parents, perfect teachers exist only in our imaginations. Warts and all, the kind of people and teachers they are in this world is what makes them real and that gives them the power to so touch and move each child who enters their classroom. Whether the student is a country boy or city girl, native son or émigré, prince or pauper, they try their hardest, sometimes struggle, to better understand each one, themselves, and how they combine the two. They do this for one reason and one reason only: So that they can educate the student and so the student can learn.

They can't do otherwise, for they are teachers.

## NOTE

1. Plato is an eighth grader in the Lincoln Junior High School in Middleville, Wisconsin.

# ABOUT THE AUTHOR

**Richard Bromfield,** Ph.D., a graduate of Bowdoin College and the University of North Carolina at Chapel Hill, is a clinical psychologist on the faculty of Harvard Medical School. He is author of *Playing for Real: Exploring the World of Play Therapy and the Inner Worlds of Children* and *Doing Child and Adolescent Psychotherapy, The Ways and Whys,* and also writes for professional and popular periodicals. Dr. Bromfield has a private practice with children and adults in both Brookline and Hamilton, Massachusetts.